BUILT ON COAL

A history of Beverly, Edmonton's working class town

by Lawrence Herzog

Dedication

To my mother Shirley and my father Wilfred, my two working class heroes, who instilled in me a respect for the past and ignited a passion to discover and tell the stories of those who have gone before.

Acknowledgements

You would not be holding this book in your hands were it not for the tireless efforts of the Beverly History Committee and countless generous citizens throughout the community. They include: Walter MacDonald, Stella Skrzekowski, Amy Bidney, Dan Vriend, Fred and Marie Nash, Ann Nicolai, Lawrence Husieff, John Yuzwenko, Harold & Joyce Jinks, Joyce McFadyen, Honore Dahlberg West, Elsie Muir and Margaret Muir Andriats, Jean and George Kozak, Olivena Horne, Tini Van Ameyde, Winnie Olthuis, Peter and Sadie Prins, Olga Hlus, Doris and Peter Kule, Mary Harasim, Donna Moffitt, Jack Campbell, Shelagh Harder, Fay Atkinson and Cornel Rusnak.

Space does not permit the printing of the names of everyone who helped out, but this book is testament to the size of their contribution. A heartfelt thank you to all area residents and past residents who gave generously of their memories, their photos and their time.

It was Shirley Lowe who believed in me enough to suggest I tackle this project. In the spirit of fair play, I insisted that she edit the result. Her abundant historical knowledge and enthusiasm for the subject were invaluable.

The staff at the City of Edmonton Archives helped with all manner of research. I am grateful for the generosity and helpful spirit of Bruce Ibsen, Patrick Lamb, Johwanna Alleyne, Kathryn Ivany, Lois Kleebaum and Virginia Hall. Retired city archivist Helen LaRose and retired reference librarian June Honey provided wisdom and encouragement when I needed it most and pointed me in the direction of little treasures.

Marlena Wyman at the Provincial Archives of Alberta was a great benefit sourcing Beverly images and geological information related to coal operations. Michael Kostek, archivist for the Edmonton Public School Board, provided valuable insight into the operation of the early schools and the more recent history of public schools in the district. The staff at the Edmonton Public Schools Archives and Museum were patient and helpful with many mysteries to solve.

Other sources included the Glenbow Alberta Institute, Photo Archive Division; Edmonton Public Library; Edmonton Journal and Edmonton Bulletin Microfilm Collection; clippings from the Beverly Page and various issues of the Highlands Historical Foundation Newsletter, especially Anita Jenkins' story on A.J. Davidson.

Dave Robb, Editor, Real Estate Weekly, generously provided desktop publishing and digitizing for a project on a tight budget. If the book looks good, it's because of the skill of Liz Bolduc, graphic designer and Dianne Price, digital imager.

I am especially grateful to Jaime Apolonio Jr., who assisted with research and organization of the sometimes overwhelming amount of paper, photographs and other material. He helped me find clarity in the clutter.

Space and budget mean that there are many stories of many people and many places that unfortunately I could not include. Perhaps a second volume . . .

Lawrence Herzog

Introduction

Like Edmonton itself, the area known as Beverly grew swiftly in the early years of the 20th century. People were drawn here by an abundance of cheap, cultivable land, proximity to the services of the burgeoning urban settlement and jobs in the coal mines below its feet.

Born of those working class roots deep underground, Beverly, like most blue collar communities, has had to fight hard for respect and its rightful share. It has been unceremoniously called "that place of shanty shacks east of Edmonton, the town where those who can't afford Edmonton live, a horrible amalgam of unlit streets, unpaved roads, undistinguished residents." In truth, municipal services like water, sewer and gas didn't come to Beverly until the boom of the 1950s but this was a community rich in many other ways.

When Beverly amalgamated with Edmonton in 1962, it brought to a conclusion a remarkable half century chapter of birth, growth and struggle. Yet, even though it's been nearly 40 years since Edmonton appended Beverly to its eastern hip, some of the endearing small town elements still survive. Beverly old timers still refer to going downtown as "a trip into the city." Beverly has been and still is a community in the truest sense of the word. This volume focuses on events before amalgamation because, in the shifting sands of time, those are the stories most at risk of being lost.

As I researched this subject over many months, it was the stories of the people that emerged as the real treasure. The names from Beverly's life as a town - Bergman, Dando, Lawton, Abbott, Prins, Hollingworth, Hunter and a hundred more - are not well known to most Albertans. But in each of their stories resonate the spirit that builds and binds every great community - hard work, determination, friendship, respect and goodwill. When 35 per cent of the Town of Beverly was on direct government relief in the depths of the Great Depression (compared with eight per cent in the province), people pulled together to help each other in a remarkable, inspirational display of the deep meaning of "community." It's no wonder Beverly inspires its citizens to stay; many of them have called it home for 40 and 50 years.

This book was born, as are most good things in Beverly, out of a tenacious sense of pride. When a small group of local residents got together in 1997 to talk about ways to celebrate and rejuvenate the community, telling the history emerged as a favoured project. And so the Beverly History Project was launched, with no immediate funding but a depth of conviction.

This little volume is the result. It is a portrait of an Alberta working class town. The heroes are the people - honest, decent, hardworking folks who brought Beverly to life and, even now, abide as its heart and soul. I hope you find as much enlightenment and inspiration reading their stories as I did researching and writing them.

Lawrence Herzog

Table of Contents

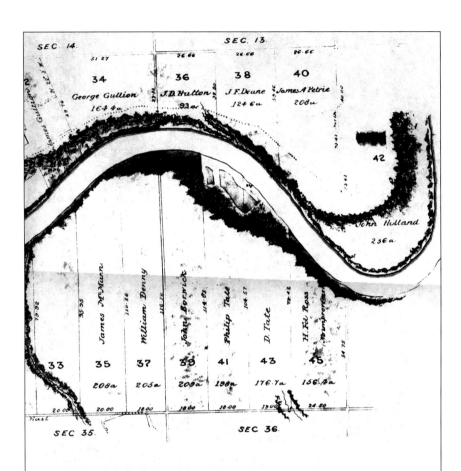

Beginnings

Clover Bar Farm

Painting by Kay Smith

According to the Geographic Board of Canada's Place-Names of Alberta, published in 1928, Beverly was named by the Canadian Pacific Railway in 1904 after Beverly township, Wentworth County, Ontario. The Ontario Beverly was the former home of R.R. Jamieson, General Superintendent of the CPR and may well have been named after Beverley, a town in Yorkshire, England.

Beverly's earliest settlers were homesteaders who laid claim to land on North Saskatchewan River Lots 36, 38, 40 and 42 comprised mostly of bush and sloughs in what was then an improvement district. Drawn by the promise of a better life and, in some cases, fleeing persecution and oppressive regimes, these settlers came from Germany, Scotland, England, Holland, Ukraine, and other European countries. Others came from the United States, drawn by the opportunity to own land at very reasonable prices. The first River Lot and township surveys, conducted in 1882, show several newcomers as owners of land in what was to become Beverly. These River Lots were owned respectively by J.D. Hutton, J.F. Deane, James Petrie and John Holland, none of whom apparently stuck around long enough to have an impact on the future community.

It wasn't until the early days of the 20th century that settlement really kicked into gear. In 1906, when Alberta was barely a year old, Beverly was incorporated as a hamlet. Word got out that this new place at the edge of the frontier was blessed both with rich black soil, ideally suited to farming and with another treasure far below the soil. When rich coal seams were discovered on the banks of the North Saskatchewan River, companies quickly invaded and the boom was on. Beverly lots became quoted in real estate deals in such far-flung quarters as England, New Zealand and Australia. By 1913, the value of assessed land in Beverly topped $3 million

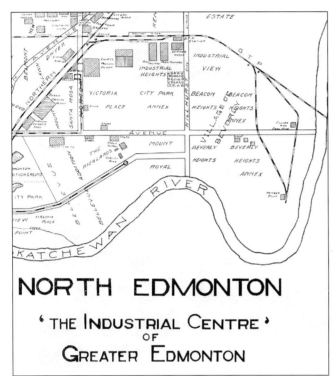

NORTH EDMONTON

'THE INDUSTRIAL CENTRE'
OF
GREATER EDMONTON

From North Edmonton Industrial Review, Published 1913

City of Edmonton Archives

However, compared with Edmonton, Beverly property remained a bargain. The city had expanded at a tremendous rate prior to World War I, stoking the engine of economic growth and driving up real estate values. Many newcomers settled in Beverly and other outlying areas as a way of decreasing their living costs and, with work in the mines, they had found what real estate promoters had called "the ideal residence section of the city." In reality, many of the earliest settlers in Beverly were making little working in the mines and couldn't afford to buy land or build houses. As in Edmonton, many of these working class folks were forced to live in tents.

Still the promoters persisted. A story in the Daily Capitol published June 13th, 1912 announced that the first lots in Beverly Heights - "a high-class subdivision fronting on the Saskatchewan river, presenting an admirable view of the stream" - had been placed on the market. "Within a few months, it will be within a few minutes walk of a street car line affording easy and quick access to the city." The story went on to assure readers that water, sewer, electric light and other conveniences would also be installed within a few months. "According to the terms of all agreements, a certain class of residences must be erected thus guaranteeing that there will be no unsuitable or unsightly dwellings," the story concluded. It was to be decades before those promises came to pass.

Another story in the May 17th, 1913 edition of the paper trumpeted Beverly Heights, Beverly Heights Annex, Beacon Heights and Beacon Heights Annex as a place of promise. "On March 27nd, 1912, Gus Buerling started work on his home out in the bush on Alberta Avenue in the face of the ridicule of his friends, but today the tables have turned and he finds himself in a thickly settled community ... with good prospects of street car service to the city, already having three grocery stores and a barber shop, five miles of street graded and contracts let for two and one-half miles more and a sidewalk from the car line to the most remote part of the subdivision."

The Coming of the Railway

The Grand Trunk Pacific Railway (GTPR) originally intended to cross the North Saskatchewan River where the High Level Bridge now stands, but the rail company was unable to reach an agreement with the Canadian Pacific Railway. With some monetary inducement from Edmonton, the railway decided instead to cross the river at Clover Bar, where the river was at its narrowest. Construction on the bridge, 1,655 feet long and 138 feet above mean low water level, commenced in 1907. Materials were transported on a spur built eastwards from the Canadian Northern Railway (CNoR) main line near modern day 66th Street and 125th Avenue. The Clover Bar Bridge was completed in 1908, a year before track was laid from the east. A substantial embankment was built to keep the track relatively level until west of a crossing at 50th Street.

Clover Bar Bridge under construction, 1908

Provincial Archives of Alberta, Ernest Brown Collection B.1535

13

Rather than crossing at grade, the GTPR decided to cross the CNoR main line (near today's 125th Avenue and 66th Street) on a wooden trestle, approached by a 0.4 per cent grade from the east. The trestle, completed in May 1909, was 1,819 feet long and 42 feet high - and so it became known as "the high line." It was removed in 1923 after the CNoR became part of Canadian National Railways (CNR) and a complex crossing and junction at grade, the East Junction, was completed.

*Clover Bar Bridge -
Ballast Train,
September 1, 1909*

City of Edmonton
Archives, EA-143-1

A map published in 1913 in the North Edmonton Industrial Review shows a Beverly Railway Station at the 50th Street crossing, but 1998 research by railway historian Alan Vanterpool indicates a Beverly station was unlikely. There was already a station at Clover Bar about three miles to the east and another at 66th St on the joint CNoR and GTPR lines, approximately four miles west of Clover Bar. None of the GTPR/CNR employee timetables from the time describe such a station, and if one existed, it is doubtful that it picked up or discharged paying passengers. A request for a Beverly Railway Station was repeatedly forwarded from successive town councils starting in 1914, but to no avail.

In the early 1900's, the GTPR became the biggest shipper of coal in the province and almost all that coal was obtained from mines on either side of the Clover Bar Bridge. The Beverly mines that supplied the railway included the Clover Bar, Humberstone and Old Bush.

The Birth of a Village

As word spread of the bounty of the soil and the bounty of coal far below, Beverly quickly grew from wide open fields and an improvement district to a bustling little community. By 1913, the population was more than 400 and a proclamation issued at Edmonton May 22nd, 1913 stated that under the village act, the area known as the "North Half of Section 12, Township 53, Range 24, west of the fourth meridian, has been erected a village under the name of Village of Beverly in the Province of Alberta." The first election for village council was held June 10th, with seven candidates vying for three positions. Elected were Mr. C.E. Davidson, Mr. A. Jordan and Mr. Robert T. Walker, who became Chairman. Walker worked as a coal miner, laundry truck driver and later elevator operator at the Beverly Coal Company. He was to again lead the town 11 years later when he was elected Mayor in 1924.

The Edmonton Bulletin in its June 14th, 1913 edition reported, "The policy as outlined by the village council is one of progress and development, and there is every indication that the village of Beverly will become a place of no small

Mundy's Map, 1912

City of Edmonton Archives
EAM-31

importance in the very near future." In its earliest days, the village comprised the subdivisions of Beacon Heights, Beacon Heights Annex, Beverly Heights and Beverly Heights Annex.

The first council meeting was held June 17th, 1913 in the Methodist Mission tent. There are indications the tent was at the time located near present day 118th Avenue and 48th Street or it may well have been situated on church land on the east side of 38th Street at the corner of 120th Avenue. At the inaugural meeting, councillors discussed difficulties with water and sidewalks - which were ongoing problems over the next many years. They also visited the issue of hiring a town constable. At later meetings that year, the possibility of $25 fines for errant cattle and horses was a topic of debate. Five thousand dollars was borrowed for construction of sidewalks, drains and

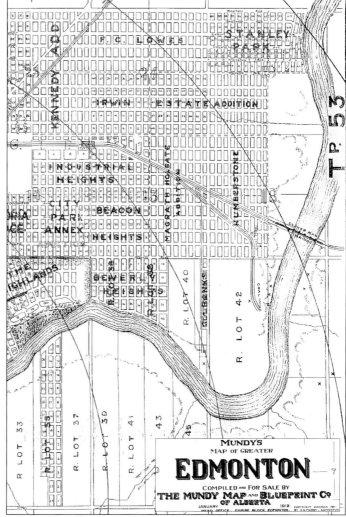

ditches and installing a culvert under Alberta Avenue (118th Avenue) at Brown Street (48th Street) to drain water.

Bylaw No. 1 authorized borrowing up to $30,000 for construction of roads and sidewalks and the purchase of fire equipment. But shortly after the debenture was put on the market, a worldwide recession struck and the needed money was never raised. As the economy and Beverly's prospects soured, even the request for a $2,000 loan was turned down by the Union Bank. This was the beginning of the community's financial struggles, which were to continue for many years. Bylaw No. 2 governed the licensing of pool and billiard rooms, which was apparently a concern for the council of the day.

Selling Beverly

Several land companies began offering lots for sale in Beverly; among them, the Robertson-Davidson Real Estate Company. This firm, established by Adam James Davidson and his brother-in-law George Robertson, was headquartered at 10012 Jasper Avenue in Edmonton. The partners purchased a huge tract of land and its mineral rights - what was then known as River Lots 36, 38 and 40 and today runs from 34th Street to 50th Street and the North Saskatchewan River to 118th Avenue. They divided part of what came to be known as Beverly Heights into lots and began selling these parcels in 1912. To make their properties more appealing, they negotiated with the City of Edmonton to extend the streetcar tracks further east from The Highlands subdivision.

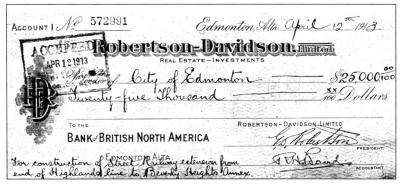

Robertson-Davidson Limited cheque, April 12, 1913

Artifact courtesy A. J. Davidson family

A cancelled cheque kept by the Davidson family to this day shows that Robertson-Davidson Limited paid the City of Edmonton $25,000 to build the streetcar line. On the cheque is written: "For construction of Street Railway extension from end of Highlands line to Beverly Heights Annex." The real estate, coal and investment brokers were bullish on the new venture, but boom went bust in 1913 and the line was never built. The City of Edmonton chose instead to provide a chartered bus service. As land prices collapsed, Robertson-Davidson Limited lost most of its remaining Beverly property to taxes, save some along the river. Robertson wanted out and so Davidson bought his share of the company and George Robertson and family moved to Los Angeles, California.

Robertson-Davidson Limited, Jasper Avenue, 1912

City of Edmonton Archives, EA-160-489

Using the mineral rights the partners had acquired with the land, Davidson started the Beverly Coal and Gravel Company in 1917. The venture was located at 36th Street and south of 104th Avenue, where Rundle Park is now. In 1928, Davidson leased the mine to the Bush Mine Company, and that was the name by which the mine was best known.

Incorporation as a Town

The little community continued to grow and as shadows of war loomed over Europe in 1914, Beverly reached a population of 1,000 - more than double the summer previous. With people pouring in, the village council moved to increase its borrowing power and petitioned the provincial municipal affairs minister to include in the village portions of some river lots. But the minister pointed out that, if he did so, the new lots would give Beverly 742 acres - 82

Artifact courtesy Mark Bergman

more than allowed for a village. Council then passed Bylaw No. 8 on April 6th, 1914 which called for the "erection of the village and land below Buckingham Avenue (108th Avenue) into a town", which is how the fledgling community got its river lots.

Aware of the need for Edmonton's support of the move, a delegation requested to appear before City Council July 9, 1914. At that meeting, Parks and Markets Commissioner A.G. Harrison told council that Beverly had 350 to 400 dwellings, stores and churches, a large public school and one manufacturing plant - Beverly Sheet and Metal Works (which was run by Robert G. Hay, who was to become Mayor in 1916). Attendance at the school was 170 and the community boasted several churches including Presbyterian, Church of England and Methodist. "There are several miles of plank sidewalks and graded roads," Harrison told council. "The village tax rate is seven mills, and the school rate is five mills, making a total of 12 mills."

He went on to explain that good drinking water could be obtained at a depth of ten to 40 feet all through the village and the widely spaced lots were valued at $250. "As the houses and buildings in the proposed town are very much scattered over a large territory, it would only be a source of expense to the City of Edmonton at the present time to extend its limits so as to take in the territory which will comprise the proposed new town, because none of the utilities, if extended, would pay expenses for some years." The official record of the Edmonton City Council meeting reads:

> *Delegate from Beverly: "We feel as a community out there that we would like benefit of the rates that are collected out there in our district, that is, we should like to be a separate quarter. Possibly some arrangement could be made between the two bodies by which the sewerage and water may be co-operated, but that would be for a committee, and if we could arrange for such a one we would be very glad."*

Ald. Clarke: "You want the rates; that is all you want for the present. There is no hard feeling between you and us? In the meantime you can go on in your own way as a town?"

Delegate: "Yes."

Commissioner Harrison made this bold prediction: "There is little doubt that at some future time, this territory will become part of the City of Edmonton." But there were too few residents in Beverly to warrant annexation then, so city council threw support behind town status instead. The headline in the Daily Capitol the next day read "INCORPORATION OF BEVERLY AS TOWN FAVORABLE TO CITY."

Beverly's incorporation, issued August 15, 1914, reads: "On the 13 day of July 1914 Town of Beverly. South 1/2 of Section 13 Township 53, Range 24, west of the 4th meridian, all of River Lots 36 and 38 Edmonton Settlement and that part of River Lot 40 Edmonton Settlement which has been subdivided and registered at the Land Titles Office under plan A.R. 2528."

Beverly's First Mayor and Council

Provincial Archives of Alberta, Ernest Brown Collection B. 6940

The incorporation didn't help with the town's economic woes. The assessment was set at $2.055 million, a 35 per cent drop from the year previous and the tax rate nearly tripled to 16 mills. A special school levy of 50 cents was applied against every lot.

The town's first municipal election was held August 3rd, with Gus Bergman topping the race for Mayor with 64 votes. Thomas Dando was next with 55 votes, Robert Hay garnered 32 and A. Jordan received 15 votes. Councillors elected were Weir, Richards, Manning, Booker, Lightfoot and Jack. A story in the August 11th, 1914 edition of the Beverly Advertiser and North Edmonton News reported the newly-

FIRST MAYOR and COUNCIL 1914-15

T. Booker
Chairman of Public Works

J.W. Lightfoot
Chairman of Health & Safety.

G.C. Bergman Mayor.
And Chairman of Finance Committee.

J. Jack

R. Weir

W. Manning

F. Richards

TOWN OF BEVERLY ALBERTA

elected council members were sworn in August 7th and held their first meeting Monday, August 10th. At that inaugural meeting, councillors discussed "restraining animals at large" and agreed to table a bylaw at their next meeting to "abate this nuisance." The newspaper report went on to say that, "Councillor Weir suggested that it is advisable to arrange for a cemetery in the neighborhood, also a park and a market."

Beverly's First Mayor

Gustave C. Bergman was born of Swedish-American parents in Paxton, Illinois on October 22nd, 1872 and raised in Lucas County, Iowa. His mother died when he was just seven years old when the carriage in which she was riding was hit by a train. His father was unable to care for him and so young Gus was forced to work from a young age. Despite a lack of formal education, he audited classes at Drake University in 1892 and the next year began work for

Gus Bergman

Provincial Archives of Alberta, Ernest Brown Collection B.6946

the Keystone View Company, selling 3-D and "stereoview" photographic viewers. As a salesman for the firm, he travelled to such far flung locations as Europe and to Canada - where he fell in love with the soon to be province of Alberta.

His grandson, Mark Bergman, says Gus rafted the Red Deer River in 1902 and, when the raft beached near what is now Erskine in Central Alberta, he laid claim to land. In Iowa, as a poor young man, he could not own land but in Canada he had found a dream come true. Alberta was soon to become a province and, as the boom began and thousands of newcomers poured in, Bergman watched with a keen eye. He knew that people would want to settle near the railway lines and so, when the Grand Trunk Pacific arrived in Edmonton, he decided to head north and buy land.

Bergman settled in Beverly sometime after 1912 and purchased 36 lots in Block

23 of the fledgling Beacon Heights subdivision on March 11th, 1913. That year, he began building a house on Brown Street, at what is now 12014 48 Street. He was elected mayor in the town's municipal vote, held August 3rd, 1914. During his term, a police force and fire brigade were established. Five months into his term at the December 14th, 1914 meeting, council voted him a salary of $25 a month. Council meetings were sometimes held at Bergman's home.

Gus & Hildur Bergman

Photo courtesy Mark Bergman

Jean Kaminsky Kozak, whose father William purchased the Bergman house on a 1.5 acre lot December 6, 1918, remembers that there was a pump for the well in the kitchen of the house, a most welcome feature for the day. Jean's sister Sue Stumph says the family members all fondly recall the end-to-end verandah which graced the front of the home. It was also one of the few houses built in the district with a concrete basement and, all these years later, the house, extensively modified, is still standing on its original location. The Kaminsky family owned the house until 1983, when mother Nancy Ochota Kaminsky passed away.

Gus and Hildur Bergman had six children - Bonita, Sybil, Meredith, Dolores, John and Earl. Bonita died when she was just a teenager from a burst appendix sustained playing basketball.

Bergman ran again for Mayor in December 1915 but was defeated by Robert G. Hay, a sheet metal worker and union organizer, 108 votes to 59. He lived in Beverly until 1917, when he moved back to the farm at Erskine. "He was as honest as the day was long," Mark Bergman remembers of his grandfather. "He used to say it was better to be born lucky than rich, and, when you consider his life, he was indeed a lucky man."

On January 5th, 1962, at the age of 89, Gus Bergman attended the ceremonies marking Beverly's amalgamation with Edmonton and said he was "perhaps the oldest man in the house - and the happiest." Mr. Bergman died just a few

*Gus Bergman's house,
12014 48th Street,
circa 1930*

Photo courtesy Jean &
George Kozak

months later and was buried in Edmonton's Beechmount Cemetery. The Bergman Sub-division, from 34th Street on the east to 50th Street on the west and from 122nd Avenue north to the CNR tracks, was named in his honour in 1987.

The Town Hall

When the provincial Department of Municipal Affairs authorized Beverly to sell up to $25,000 worth of debentures in 1915, the town at long last had enough money to build a town hall. But wrangles over the land, owned by the Robertson-Davidson Company, held up the project well into 1918. There are indications the issue was put to a plebiscite in February 1917 and finally town council approved the purchase of 12 lots fronting the north side of 118th Avenue for $6,000.

Allan Merrick Jeffers

City of Edmonton Archives

The two-storey municipal building was designed by renowned architect Allan Merrick Jeffers, also the mastermind of the Alberta Legislature. Besides the ornate, American Beaux-Arts influenced Legislature, Jeffers was also responsible for a number of other government buildings early this century. Jeffers was born February 8th, 1875 in Pawtucket, Rhode Island and trained as an architect before being elected in 1898 to the Rhode Island State Legislature, a structure that bears striking resemblance to the Alberta Legislature.

During this time, Jeffers' entered several design competitions. His daughter, Claire Chase, says he won two - one in France and the other for the Alberta Legislature. Chase suggests her father decided on Alberta because designing a new building for a new province seemed a greater challenge. Jeffers came to

Edmonton in April 1907 and became Chief Architectural Draughtsman for the Alberta Department of Public Works on May 1st, 1907.

And then, just as suddenly as he came, he left, moving to California in 1923. Historian Michael Payne, writing in Alberta Past in 1994, noted that there has been considerable speculation over the years about exactly why Jeffers departed Edmonton. Some theorize there was no more work for architects specializing in large public buildings. Others have suggested that Jeffers was lured by the bright lights of Hollywood and the opportunity to design movie sets. His family asserts that the reasons were personal. Whatever the case, the fact is that he lived in Alberta just 16 years, but left a mark that has lasted more than a lifetime, even putting his stamp on little Beverly.

Jeffers' design for the Town Hall was scaled down by a penny conscious council and budgeted at $7,239, including $125 for a vault door. The building was constructed by Brown & Hargrave Contractors, based at 1 Merchants Bank Building in downtown Edmonton. It was completed early in 1918 but problems with the building quickly arose and council minutes from 1918 indicate concern over several defects.

The structure at 3806 Alberta Avenue (118th Avenue) housed police, court and fire services on the main floor, with a dance hall and schoolroom for Grades

Election Day in Beverly, February 1934, when Town Hall was still two stories

City of Edmonton Archives, EA-160-889

23

One and Two on the top floor. The jail was in a separate building on the site and behind it was a corral to hold stray cattle and horses. Among noteworthy people connected with the town hall was Emily Murphy, who served as Justice of the Peace in Beverly.

Cracks began appearing in the brick walls of the Town Hall during the Depression years and in 1936 safety concerns prompted councillors to commission a structural analysis. The building inspector T. Thornton recommended tie rods be placed across the front of the building below the second ceiling and two rods be tied with turnbuckles under the ceiling of the roof partition. Thornton also suggested that "citizens of Beverly refrain from using the auditorium for dances."

While dancing had impacted the integrity of the structure, the Depression had destroyed the economic footings of the town itself. Beverly declared bankruptcy and, because it was deemed too expensive to demolish the hall, only the top storey was removed. The fire and police services remained in the building. The province replaced the town council with an administrator in 1937 and in 1949, when the Beverly Mayor and Town Council were reinstated, the town hall again served as the seat of the civic government. An expansion in 1950/51 added two police cells and a police office.

Beverly Town Hall, reduced to one storey circa 1968

City of Edmonton Archives, EA-20-5109

The hall closed for good at the end of January 1962, the month after amalgamation with the City of Edmonton. It stood for a few more years and then was demolished. For a time the land sat vacant while Beverly citizens encouraged the city and the province to build a community facility on the site that had been the seat of government for so long. The province responded by erecting an Alberta Liquor Control Board outlet, which closed a few years ago when retail sales of alcohol were privatized by the Conservative government.

Difficult Days

As 1915 wound down, the town found itself running a hefty deficit. Land seized for non-payment of taxes was sold in January 1917 - with 46 blocks selling for an average of $20. The same lots in 1914 were selling for upwards of $500. Thomas R. Dando replaced Robert Hay as Mayor in 1918, but the economic skid couldn't be stopped. Beverly's population had dwindled to 1000, and the town was barely existing on its taxes and coal revenues.

Water, Water Everywhere

Early reports of Beverly often speak of the abundant water, which was both a blessing and a curse. "The best of water can be reached at a depth of less than 15 feet," reported the Daily Capitol in a story May 17th, 1913. "This water is claimed by the citizens to be much better than the city water." But the high water table made for difficult building and travel and horrifically muddy roads quickly became a way of life - a way of life that was to persist for the next 40 years.

Envelope No. 1

Edmonton, Alta. *Dec. 7* 1913

I hereby promise to contribute $ *25 Cents*

per week during the year 191 *3* to the current expense of the Beverly Methodist Church.

Name *C. E. Davidson*

Street Address *Beverly Boulevard*

Artifact courtesy
Joyce McFadyen,
Beverly United Church

Mud was ankle and even knee deep and early vehicles just weren't able to handle the challenging conditions. To help people get around, wooden sidewalks were constructed along several thoroughfares, including Agnes and Westminister Avenues (115th and 121st Avenues) and Chaplain (40th Street), Henry (44th Street), Race (38th Street) and Appleton (42nd Street) Streets. The Robertson Davidson company lent council $5,000 for the construction of a sidewalk along Knox (114th) Avenue.

Contractor Malcolm McCrimmon and three others were hired in April 1916 to construct the early Beverly thorough fares, including Alberta Avenue (118th Avenue), Knox (114th Avenue) and Beverly Boulevard (38th Street south of 118th Avenue). The tender values were: $4,617 to Mr. McCrimmon, $4,708 to James Kerr, $4,728 to T. Griffin and $5,050 to J. Radford. "Beverly now boasts two first class streets connecting with the city," reported the June 26, 1916 edition of the Edmonton Bulletin. The paper related that a new six-foot wide (wooden) sidewalk had been constructed on Alberta, with four foot wide sidewalks alongside the other two roadways.

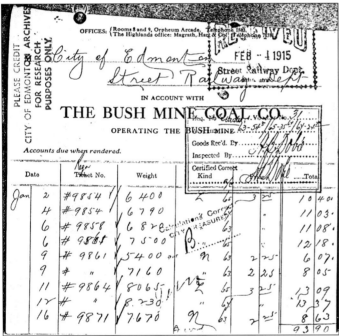

City of Edmonton Archives

Beverly Public Library

Bylaw No. 35, passed by town council February 21, 1916, established the Public Library. Over the years, the library was located in several places, including the Central School and the Town Hall. In the 1930s, the library was operated out of the basement of the United Church and managed by Dorothy and Abraham Abbott. For their efforts, Dorothy was paid $6.50 every three months while Abraham received $3.25.

Beverly Cottage and Returned Soldiers Rest

By early 1916, more than 130 Beverly citizens had enlisted for military service and, with some of them returning home wounded from the battlefront, the need for a local hospital was identified. The Cottage Hospital and Returned Soldiers' Bureau was established in 1916. President of the Board was Mrs. Beata Humberstone and the hospital was financed through grants from town council, the Beverly School Board, public subscriptions of $250 and donations of local merchants. The facility was overseen by Annie Winter of the Victorian Order of Nurses, working under the direction of the medical health officer, Dr. Atkinson. When the 1918 Spanish influenza epidemic swept through Edmonton, taking hundreds of lives, Dr. Atkinson, Nurse Taylor and other caring citizens were credited with saving many lives through their devotion.

Limping through the 1920s

Frederick C. Humberstone, the younger brother of noted Edmonton coal baron William Humberstone, was born in Newton Brook, Ontario in 1857 and so that made him 62 years old when he was elected Mayor of Beverly in January 1920. For Frederick, his win in Beverly was third time lucky; in 1910 and 1916 he had been an unsuccessful candidate for Edmonton City Council, running on a platform of selling public utilities to private business. He is unique among Beverly's mayors on at least two counts: he was the only large scale businessman to be elected and the only one to die in office. After Frederick Humberstone's death in February 1921, Robert Weir became Beverly Mayor.

Beverly limped along through the 1920s, subsisting on the employment provided by the coal mines including the Humberstone, Bush and the cross-river mines in Clover Bar like the Ottewell (known by residents as the Clover Bar), Black Diamond Mine, Fraser-Mackay Collieries and Marcus Collieries. In the ten years between 1920 and 1930, successive councils each left the town a little deeper in debt. When the Great Depression struck, Beverly was already flat on its back.

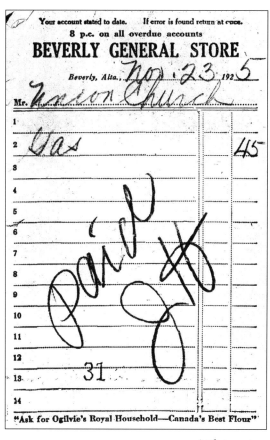

Artifact courtesy
Joyce McFadyen,
Beverly United Church

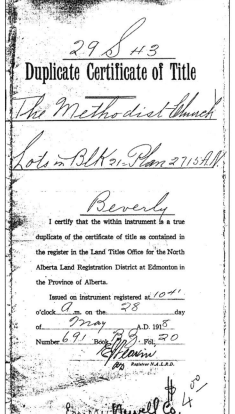

Artifact courtesy
Beverly United Church

Prins Family, circa 1925

Photo courtesy Prins Family

The People

Samuel Hoyle, Bush Coal miner, 1937

Thousands of immigrants poured into the Edmonton area between 1870 and 1914. During that time, Edmonton's population catapulted from barely 100 to more than 72,000, with a tripling in just the three years between 1911 and 1914. These settlers came primarily from Eastern Canada, Europe and the United States; a diverse collection of cultures, languages and traditions. And yet, with abundant resources, what seemed boundless possibilities for growth and a vigour that only a new and growing community can generate, they forged a prosperous and remarkably harmonious place.

As the land boom pushed prices in Edmonton upward, Beverly gained appeal as a low cost alternative. Anglo Saxons settled largely south of 118th Avenue, while newcomers from Eastern Europe and the Baltic States preferred the area north of the avenue. There was no power, no water, initially no railway and few roads, but the price was right and there was employment at the local mines and in the packing plants that were building north near the Fort Trail. It was a formula for sustenance, growth and entrepreneurship; a place to live humbly or think big. Here are a few of their stories.

The Davidson Family

Adam James Davidson, or A.J. as he was known, arrived in the Beverly area in 1912, drawn by the land boom. He and his brother-in-law George Robertson formed the Robertson-Davidson Real Estate Company and were the first developers of what is known as Beverly Heights. The boom went bust the following year and the partners lost much of the land to property taxes. In true pioneering spirit and entrepreneurial zeal, Davidson merely picked himself up, dusted off and went onto other ventures, making his family's pursuit of golden opportunity come true, just like the early 20th century newspaper advertisements had promised it would.

A. J. Davidson 1913

Photo courtesy Doris Gibbs and the Davidson Family

Davidson was born in Galt (now Cambridge) Ontario of Scottish parents on May 19, 1864. He married Isabella McLauchlan Smith on January 6, 1892 and the couple had five children between 1893 and 1903 - Cora Bell, Louis Harold, George Gordon, Jean Marguerite and James Robin. In 1910, at the age of 46, A.J. decided to leave behind their comfortable life in Galt and see for himself whether all the adventurous stories of the "Last Best West" were true. On the advice of his brother who had preceded him west, A.J. and his 16-year-old son Louis claimed a homestead near Hanna, Alberta. Isabella and the other children soon followed and the family split its time between Hanna and Calgary so the children could obtain a good education.

The family joined A.J. in Edmonton in 1913 and they rented the Frank Oliver house on 103rd Street near 100th Avenue. The family then purchased a property at 10011 113 Street. With the collapse of property values, A.J. may well have needed to find other means of paying the bills or perhaps he just knew a good business opportunity for during the First World War, he became a shareholder of Western Foundry and Machine. This munitions factory which made shells and other ammunition for the war, was located at 53rd Street and 124th Avenue, adjacent to the Canadian National Railway tracks. In 1920 A.J.

and Isabella rented a house from William Magrath at 5650 Ada Boulevard to be closer to his Beverly Coal and Gravel Company operation off 36th Street and 104th Avenue.

The house was one of the most lavish erected during Magrath Holgate Company's 1912 push to develop The Highlands and it still stands in its original location. The Davidson family called it "The Big House." In 1924 A.J. bought the house

Davidson family and house, circa 1938

Photo courtesy Doris Gibbs and the Davidson Family

from Ada Magrath, then a widow, for $10,000 and some shares in Western Foundry. The family was to own the house until 1982.

As natural gas began to gain in popularity, A.J. may well have foreseen a softening in the market for coal or perhaps, with advancing age, he decided to get out of the coal business and leave it to younger men. He leased the mine to Bush Mine Company and diversified into dairy farming - a love it seems he had never lost from days growing up as a boy on a dairy farm in Ontario. The barn that had been built for horses working the mine property became home to a herd of purebred Holstein Friesian cattle and, after expansion, it accommodated 30 head of milking cows and another 30 head of young stock, dry stock and bulls. A.J. opened up 180-acres as pastureland and the superb facility and careful breeding produced many awards at exhibitions in Edmonton, Red Deer, Calgary and Saskatoon. As A.J. reached his seventies and began to slow down, his son Gord took over operation of the dairy farm, with its distinctive red-roofed, white painted buildings.

When A.J. died on July 15, 1945 at the age of 81, his prize-winning purebred herd numbered 69. His obituary noted he was known for his public spirit and interest in civic affairs, his presidency of the Provincial Holstein Friesian

Breeders' Association and his instrumental role in the development of Beverly. Tom Hays, an Alberta cattle breeder who had worked on the Davidson dairy farm, eventually purchased the herd and flew the cattle to Argentina to improve breeding stock there. Isabella passed away April 28, 1949 at the age of 84 and Cora and her husband Glen moved into "The Big House," where they stayed until 1982. Today, houses sit where the mine and farm used to be and A.J.'s cow pastures are part of Rundle Park.

Davidson Farm, The Highlands, circa 1930s

Photo courtesy Doris Gibbs and the Davidson Family

Jessie and Mike Plesuk

When Jessie and Mike Plesuk arrived in Beverly from their native Ukraine in 1915, there was so much bush that, as Jessie tells it: "I had to find him by calling. There was no lights, no water, no roads, nothing." The couple bought a four-room wooden house from a woman who wanted to return to her homeland and transported it by horse team, little by little, to their 10-acre property along what is now 43rd Street north of 122nd Avenue. In all, it took three weeks.

Mike worked wherever he could - the railway, the coal mines, the Canada Creosoting Plant. Wages at the plant were 35 cents to 49 cents an hour. During the Great Depression, the Plesuk's six children - Bill, George, Alex, Tilly, Margie and Mike Jr.- dug potatoes all day and were rewarded with $125 for every railway box car they could fill. The strenuous labour took its toll and, in 1941, Mike Sr. died of a heart condition. He was only 53. But Jessie remained on the land and lived in the house at 12233 43 Street until the city purchased the property in 1975 for $200,000. Much of where they used to farm now resides under Yellowhead Trail. Mrs. Plesuk died in 1989 at the age of 98.

The Thomsons and The Scots

James Thomson and five other men from Scotland emigrated to Canada in the spring of 1913. Thomson, Sandy Dawson and Al Saddler settled in Beverly, attracted perhaps by the fledgling community's more affordable housing costs, while two others choose the inner city and another decided to live in The Highlands. Thomson was a carpenter by trade and so it's not surprising to learn that he built his house and helped the others build theirs before the families were brought from Scotland in June 1914. James, wife Charlotte, daughter Margaret and son Alex settled at 3620 115 Avenue, where they were to live until the mid-1940s. The original house still survives, albeit with a few additions.

They had two more daughters, Janet and Betty, and James worked at the Humberstone Coal Mine in the winter months from 1916 to 1920. He also served on Beverly Town Council in the early 1920s and, for a dozen years, spent his spring and summer working for the Northern Boat Building Company at the Highlands shop, constructing vessels for the RCMP and other clients. He was then hired by the Hudson's Bay Company to build barges and boats at Fort McMurray which carried freight down the Athabasca River to Aklavik. But he never lost his roots in Beverly and, until his death in 1945 at age 60 he and Charlotte kept their house. Charlotte sold the house in 1946 and, in more recent years, only Margaret has kept a connection to the old community.

James Thomson (third from right) and builders

Photo courtesy
Alex Thomson and
Shirley Barner

All these years later, Alex Thomson says he can still remember his father's prowess with tools and with his pipe. "He always had a pipe in his mouth," he laughs. "And he never lost the connections to the homeland. He lived in Canada but only smoked Scottish pipe tobacco and never lost his Scottish brogue."

The Nimeck Family

When Myron (Michael) Nimeck retired from coal mining in 1955, it was the end of a 54 year career working in the mines. Nimeck was born in Ukraine in 1888 and emigrated to Canada with an uncle when he was just 13. That year, he began working in coal mines and, before Beverly, he laboured at the Brule Mines near Jasper National Park.

While visiting relatives in Saskatchewan in 1918, Michael met Agnes and the two fell quickly in love. They were married within a month and returned to the Brule Mines where the newlyweds moved into a tent house (a structure with a wooden floor and sides and a canvas roof). Their first son, John, was born in that tent March 15, 1919, the day after Agnes' 17th birthday. A second son, Frank, was born June 18, 1920.

In 1923, Michael was offered a job at Beverly's Humberstone Mine as a check weighman and the family moved into a converted granary on mine property. That year, Lillian was born but she died just four months later. Another daughter, Irene MacLowick, was born November 5, 1925 and with the family growing, Michael and Agnes decided to build a house of their own.

Michael & Agnes
Nimeck Wedding Photo
May 26, 1918

Photo courtesy
Irene MacLowick

The two-room structure was constructed at the corner of 48th Street and 119th Avenue - property that, all these years later, remains in the family. John Nimeck recalls that "Beverly in those days was a town of coal miners who had big acreage gardens during summer layoffs."

More children followed: Emily on March 27, 1927; Lily Bedniak on December 20, 1929 and Maxwell on October 20, 1932. "Can you imagine seven of us living in that two room house?" Irene asks. "And there were no services - no running water, outdoor toilet, coal oil lamps." Two years later, Frankie died at age 14 from rheumatic fever and, in the depths of the Great Depression, the family didn't have the money to give him a proper funeral. The people of Beverly collected $180 to help with funeral expenses.

Nimeck Family, 1947
Back row (from left):
John, Lily, Max, Irene
Front row (from left):
Emily, Agnes, Mike

Photo courtesy
Irene MacLowick

As times improved, the family built a new six-room house at 11840 48th Street. The yard was renowned for Mike's massive greenhouse, which he constructed himself from salvage. Like other Beverly families, they had two cows, but no pigs or chickens. "Dad didn't want them," Irene remembers. The children grew up and some moved away but others have stayed in Beverly all these years. Their papa Michael passed away April 12, 1965 at the age of 77. Mamma Agnes lived another 20 years and died January 5, 1984 at the age of 81.

Nimeck Family Home,
11840 - 48 Street,
circa 1940

Photo courtesy
Irene MacLowick

Jacob & Aafje Prins in their dining room, circa 1945

Photo courtesy
Prins Family

Jacob Prins and the Dutch in Beverly

His given name was Jacob but, to the many Dutch he helped build a new life in Alberta, he was "Dad." Jacob Prins was born in Andyk (North Holland) on May 20, 1886 and from a young age was drawn to agriculture. He grew potatoes, garden seeds and tulip bulbs. When he and his wife Aafje decided to emigrate, they owned a flourishing business and were the proud parents of eight children: George, Simon, Norman, John, Peter, Winnie (Olthuis), Dorothy (Fennema), and Tina (Ellen). But little Holland was getting crowded and Jacob and Aafje decided their children would find greater opportunity in Canada. The Prins family and Aafje's brother Simon Groot, Simon's wife and eight children left Andyk on March 7, 1927, and arrived in Edmonton 19 days later. They lived first in the Christian Reformed Church at 105th Avenue and 93rd Street and Jacob began looking for property. After careful consideration, he purchased the 186-acre Humberstone Farm, nestled in a broad bend of the North Saskatchewan River and atop the Humberstone Coal Mine.

The purchase came with two bonuses: the mineral rights to the land and a large two-storey white house that William Humberstone had built as a rooming house for the coal miners.

Using the water of the North Saskatchewan to irrigate his fields, the family grew potatoes and a variety of vegetables, including cauliflower, which was an

Alberta first. As commodity prices collapsed, the Prins family began collecting royalties from the coal that others mined from the riverbank on their land. Living atop abandoned coal mines had its perils and on several occasions livestock was lost as the earth collapsed into an old shaft.

Delighted at the prosperity of their new life in Canada, Jacob Prins began encouraging other Dutch to emigrate and, when three families arrived from the Netherlands in 1936, he found farms for them to live and work near Lacombe, Alberta. When more families followed, he found it necessary to scout other locations and this turned out to be the start of a remarkable career. Prins often contacted the Canadian National Railway for information on available land parcels and, in the winter of 1937, the railway sent him to Holland to promote emigration to Western Canada. After World War II, the Christian Reformed Church's Synodical Committee appointed him Fieldman for Central British Columbia. The railway even provided Prins with a pass to travel freely in the west and, on one of those trips searching for locations suitable for Dutch farmers, he discovered the Bulkley Valley in the northern part of Central BC. It was ideally situated on the railway from Edmonton to Prince Rupert, where settlers would be assured of work in the lumber industry during winter months. Many Dutch families subsequently settled in the communities of Smithers, Terrace, Houston and Telkwa, BC.

The Prins house, circa 1940

Photo courtesy
Prins Family

Prins' message to prospective immigrants was succinct: work hard and you will succeed in Canada. During the Second World War, immigration from Europe came to a standstill, which provided Jacob with more time for his farm, but he kept an eye on future possibilities. He expected a great influx when the war ended, and he was, of course,

correct. He assisted many hundreds of newcomers, advising them, guiding them to their destination. Over the years, hundreds of tired and timid immigrants were brought to the Humberstone Farm by Jacob Prins. The hospitality of the big white Beverly house with the lilac hedges became famous on both sides of the Atlantic.

Aafje died in 1949 and her daughter-in-law Ann Prins stepped in to help with the workload, getting up before daybreak to prepare a meal for hungry travellers en route to British Columbia. Jacob Prins received no remuneration and, for a long while, paid expenses out of his own pocket. Until 1960, when he had to resign on doctor's orders, Prins travelled once a month to B.C. to check up on "his" people. Through his efforts, more than 800 Dutch families were welcomed to Canada and many settled in the Beverly area.

Over the years, the farm was expanded to more than 400 acres and was tended by the Prins' children. In the 1950s, the family tried strip mining coal on part of the property but, with the booming oil sector and a diminishing demand for coal, the venture proved unprofitable. The strip mines were the beginning of the Beverly Dump.

Working on the Prins Farm, circa 1938

Photo courtesy Prins Family

Jacob Prins passed peacefully away on April 12, 1963, while reading a book in Mother Prins' favourite corner. The funeral service filled First Christian

Tilling on the Prins Farm, circa 1938

Photo courtesy Prins Family

Reformed Church to overflowing as people travelled from all over Alberta and B.C. to pay final respects. Rev. Winston Boelkins quoted from Isaiah 54, offering the words: "Though the mountains be shaken and the hills be moved, My loving kindness for you will not be shaken nor My covenant of peace be removed, says the Lord who has compassion on you." A fitting tribute to a man who lived his life in the service of others.

The Humberstone Farm ceased vegetable production in 1966 and the land was swallowed by the birth of the Rundle Heights subdivision, the Beverly Dump and, more recently, Rundle Park. The white house, home to two generations of the Prins family, was pulled down in 1969. In 1983, the City of Edmonton named a park at 121st Avenue and 53rd Street "Jacob Prins Park" in recognition of his contribution to the area .

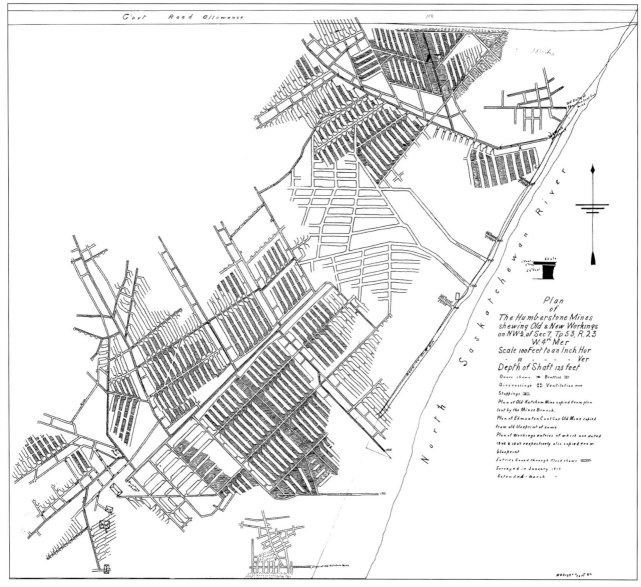

*Humberstone Mine
map, January 1919*

City of Edmonton
Archives EAM-233

Coal!

Humberstone Coal Miners, 1916

Beverly owes its early growth to events more than 70 million years ago. In those distant geological times of the Cretaceous period, much of the earth was covered with profuse vegetation flourishing in swamps. As the vegetation died and decomposed, it produced peat bogs and formed carbon. Over many years, layers of sand and mud settled from the water over some of the peat deposits. The pressure of these overlying layers, movements of the earth's crust and sometimes volcanic heat, combined to compress and harden the deposits, eventually producing the coal that put Beverly on the map.

In Beverly and around Edmonton, the seams of these undisturbed layers of transformed plant remains are up to three meters thick, although one to two meters is more typical. Edmonton coal is sub-bituminous in rank, low in ash and burns for a long while with a bright flame; with a water concentration averaging 22 per cent, if the water evaporates, the coal crumbles into a grade known as "slack." More than 95 percent of the 13 million tonnes of coal produced in Edmonton between 1874 and 1970 came from the Clover Bar seam. This seam is exposed at river level downstream from modern-day Rundle Park, near the Rundle - Gold Bar footbridge.

Coal horses, 1947

City of Edmonton
Archives, EA-600-600e

Coal mining in Edmonton was started by the Hudson's Bay Company as early as the 1840s. John Walter, boatbuilder, ferryman and Edmonton's first industrialist, imported the first coal stove in 1874 and, as settlers arrived, they needed coal to heat their flimsy wooden homes. The earliest significant mining in the area began in the early 1880s. In 1882, farmer C. Stewart employed William Humberstone to open the seam on his property, alongside the North Saskatchewan River just below where the Rundle Golf Course is now situated. The seam was found to be burned out. In March 1894, the Edmonton Bulletin reported that W.J. Graham had "recently opened a new coal drift on a seam about three miles down the river from town. Coal of very superior quality; seam five feet thick. Partly below river level; workable in winter time." The exact location of the mine remains uncertain, although there are indications it may have been in the vicinity of the Clover Bar Mine, which was to open in 1897.

Coal mined in Beverly was almost all taken from underground and much of it came from deep seams. Because it was on average a metre thick, miners spent most of their time on their knees. Far below ground, in the dark cool and damp, these workers toiled long hours in harrowing conditions. The work was strenuous and dangerous and there were a number of injuries and fatalities in Edmonton area mines. A big challenge for underground miners was, and is, a safe, orderly collapse of the roof. One of the methods utilized in the early days of the 20th century was the room-and-pillar system, where miners extracted a large rectangle of coal (a room), leaving pillars of coal to take the weight and then evacuating before the roof cracked and crashed down. Another method, not as frequently used, is the longwall system, where a face 100 to 300 feet long is mined by about 30 workers at once.

The coal was usually transported in rail cars to the foot of the shaft or slope by horses such as Welsh ponies. The production from the earliest mines was delivered to local customers by horse drawn wagon and so they came to be known as "team mines." In those days, the coal was used mostly for domestic heating in area homes. With the arrival of the railways, larger mines were able to expand aggressively and Edmonton coal was shipped as far east as Manitoba and westward into British Columbia.

As word got out about Beverly's hard, abundant coal, dozens of prospectors arrived, aiming to stake their claim along the river bank. A report in a January 1895 edition of the Edmonton Bulletin stated that "a seam of excellent coal is being mined on C. Stewart's farm on the north side of the river opposite Clover Bar." Information compiled by Richard Spence and reported in his 1971 book Atlas of Coal Mine Workings in Edmonton and Area indicates it is probable that these workings were opened up before 1894 and that mining continued on Stewart's farm at least until William Humberstone bought the property in 1899.

During the last years of the 19th century, several other mines were functioning in the vicinity, including those operated by Alex Macdonald, P. Linklater and two gentlemen named Elliott and Louisberg. At the western end of Beverly along the river, several operators started small operations between 1897 and 1904. Among them was George Hutton, who ran the Christie Mine along the north bank of the river just south of modern day Ada Boulevard and 48th Street starting in 1897 and the adjacent Trimble Mine, whose operator remains uncertain.

Mineshaft, Prins' property, circa 1940

Photo courtesy Prins Family

More than 20 coal operations are documented as operating in Beverly in the first 50 years of the 20th century, but the actual number is undoubtedly higher because there were many more tiny and ephemeral mines - most of them seasonal ventures. These small scale mines, which usually started on the side of the river bank and followed the seam into the bank, were sometimes called "gopher holes." However, the big Beverly mines and their counterparts on the east side of the North

Saskatchewan River were much more than meager diggings into the side of the slope. These extensive operations provided much of Beverly's early employment. The coal taken from the mines warmed its citizens and gave Beverly a place shared only by coal towns in the socio-economic fabric of the province.

Humberstone Coal Company

1899/1900 to 1925 and 1928 to 1934. Mine No. 43. North half, Sec 7-53-23-W4, west of river, and part of River Lot 40. Entrances along northeast bank of North Saskatchewan (30th Street) north of 111th Avenue and south of 115th Avenue. Recorded production (33 years of 34): 980,837 tons. Recovery: 47.5 per cent. Thickness of coal mined: 5 feet to 7 feet 6 inches.

William Humberstone was born to English parents in 1836 near Toronto and headed west sometime in the late 1870s. Even though he was 44 years old, he walked from Winnipeg's Fort Garry with his ox and Red River cart and the journey across the vast prairie and parkland took about three months. He arrived in Edmonton, a settlement of barely 250 persons, in October 1880. The next winter this hopeful, ambitious newcomer began pulling coal from a drift mine on the North Saskatchewan River embankment at Grierson Hill and the Humberstone Brick & Coal Company was born.

In the spring of 1899 he married Beata and that summer the North Saskatchewan River flooded, carrying their buildings and equipment down the river and laying ruin to the mine operation. The following year, Humberstone bought a half section of River Lot 42 east of what is now 34th Street and south of 118th Avenue. The Humberstone Coal Company had as its partners William J. Humberstone, C.G. Sheldon (who also managed the mine) and W.G. Heeley.

William Humberstone, circa 1880

City of Edmonton Archives, EA-10-689.61

The mine's hoisting shaft was 107 feet deep and workings extended from the river west to modern day 35th Street, south to 110th Avenue and north to 118th Avenue. As early as 1901, fire was reported at several places in the seam, and such fires continued throughout the life of the mine.

While William and his wife, Beata ran the mine, his younger brother Fred operated the farm which provided feed for the mining horses and produce for the miners who boarded on the farm. (Fred went on to become the Mayor of Beverly in 1920 and died while still in office in 1921). With William well into his seventies by 1910, Beata, 20 years his junior, began to assume more control over the day-to-day operations of the mine. She reorganized the company, speeding up growth and production and purchased, as the Edmonton Bulletin reported in 1911, new

Humberstone Coal Company Ltd., circa 1904

City of Edmonton Archives, EA-10-2718

machinery which included a compressor, coal cutters and boilers. "The new equipment not only allows a larger quantity of coal to be mined but it also assists in the economy of operation and allows the company to enter competitive fields and to take contracts for large consignments at a lower price than firms with fewer modern conveniences can give," the newspaper said.

The mine produced, as the Bulletin called it, "A high grade lignite coal which is suitable for either domestic or steam purposes." The coal was loaded onto railway cars, hauled up the spur line to the Grand Trunk Pacific (Canadian National Railways) mainline and then into the centre of the city. Production at the mine in 1910 was quoted as being between 180 tons to 200 tons a day, and the Bulletin reported the expansion would enable that capacity to be tripled in the winter of 1911-12. "A crew of

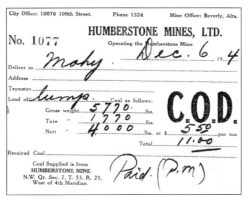

Humberstone Mines Ltd. receipt, December 6, 1904

Artifact courtesy Beverly Methodist Church

William Humberstone's farm house, 1906

Photo courtesy Prins Family

fifty men has been employed and last winter two shifts a day were utilized. It is expected that three crews may be employed this season and that as high as six hundred tons will be taken from the mines."

The Bulletin article concluded by saying: "The Humberstone Company, working property of this kind adjacent to Edmonton, has done much to call attention to the resources of this vicinity, its progressive methods have illustrated the ambitious and hopeful spirit of our capitalists. It is an industry that, pushed forward as is now being done, will undoubtedly be profitable for those concerned, and the employment it will furnish will effect beneficially many business circles in our city."

An advertisement in the June 17, 1916 edition of the Edmonton Bulletin trumpeted the features of Humberstone's mine. Manager C.G. Sheldon was quoted, calling the plant "one of the most up-to-date in the country being equipped with private electric lighting system, compressed air for machine

Humberstone Coal Miners, 1916

Glenbow Archives, Calgary, Canada NC-6-2154

mining and the latest type of shaker screen." In 1918, the mine employed more than 200 men and the monthly payroll was $25,000.

Over the years, several incidents punctuated the operation, sometimes making newspaper headlines. In 1915 and again in 1917, water broke into the shaft mine and flooded it, apparently caused by pillar-pulling that triggered caving to the surface.

William Humberstone died April 2, 1922 at the age of 86. Following his death,

the company reorganized in May 1923 under the name of Humberstone Mines Limited with an authorized capital of $30,000 or 3,000 shares of $10 each. The new money didn't help for long. A mine fire in 1925 and a depleted coal reserve were factors which contributed to the closure of his coal mine. It opened again in 1928 and continued operation until 1934, when the Depression took its toll. The mines were abandoned, with old coal carts and railway tracks left in their place and the fire left to burn out - or on. In his Atlas of Coal Mine Workings in Edmonton and Area, Richard Spence observed, "It would not be surprising if fire still smouldered in some part of the waste in these workings." Years later, the old coal mine tunnels served as a septic system for the Town of Beverly.

The First Load of Coal Ever Delivered in Edmonton.

HUMBERSTONE COAL

Humberstone Coal has satisfactorily supplied the demand for high-grade coal for steam and domestic use for over 35 years.

Sold by Ton, Load, or Carload.

BEST LUMP COAL, per ton $3.75

BEST KITCHEN COAL, per ton $3.00

Single Ton Deliveries ....25c Extra

Humberstone Coal Co.

9981 JASPER AVE.

Phones 2248—1492

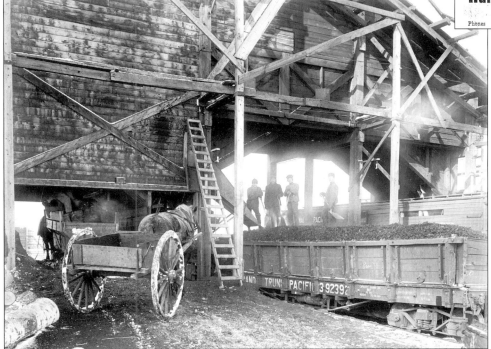

*Clover Bar Coal
Company, circa 1907*

Provincial Archives of
Alberta, Ernest Brown
Collection
B. 1598

Clover Bar Mines

*1897 (or earlier) to 1923. Mines No. 9, 11, 14,
19, 22, 79. Location: Near the river bank north
of modern day 116th Avenue to Yellowhead Trail
and westward to 34th Street. Entrances near
modern day Highway 16 East at about 28th
Street. Recorded production (23 years of 27):
357,027 tons. Recovery: 47.5 per cent.
Estimated average thickness of coal mined: 6 feet
3 inches.*

While it is no longer possible to
determine the exact location of the
workings, it is known that six mines were consolidated into No. 9 before 1905.
The hoist shaft was 85 feet deep and roughly 1,000 feet south of the Grand
Trunk Pacific Railway (GTPR) main line and 2,000 feet east of 34th Street. In
1907 the mine inspector reported that there had been fire in part of the seam
for years. A surface fire in 1909, not related to the seam fire, destroyed the
surface plant and resulted in the cave-in
of the first southern hoisting shaft. The
mine entrance was relocated after the
GTPR arrived in 1909 to be better
served by a railway spur.

*Clover Bar Coal
Company, Hauling
Room, circa 1907*

Provincial Archives of
Alberta, Ernest Brown
Collection
B. 1621

The Clover Bar Mine was the subject of
some of the finest coal mining
photographs taken by a photographer
in the formative years of the 20th
century. Several images, including
those pictured here, were captured by
renowned Edmonton photographer Ernest Brown and are now part of the
collection at the Provincial Archives of Alberta.

Beverly resident Margaret Young remembers going inside the Clover Bar Mine
with her father when she was just a little girl in the 1920s. She was fascinated
by the coal mine horses which seldom saw daylight. She says, "I used to have

a little treat for the horse. Going inside, it was cool and damp and with the water dripping and the smell of the shaft, it was quite a deal."

Old Bush Mine

1905 to 1925. Mine No. 46. Location: River Lot 42 and part of River Lot 40. Entrances near modern day 29th Street and 107th Avenue, 29th Street and 106th Avenue and 29th Street and 108th Avenue (Rundle Park). Recorded production - No. 1 Workings (seven years of nine): 40,848. No.2 Workings (12 years of 12): 486,663. Estimated average recovery; No. 1: 25 per cent. No. 2: 55 per cent. Estimated average thickness of coal mined: 5 feet 6 inches to 5 feet 9 inches.

This mine had two sets of workings - the first one was active between 1905 and 1914 and the second one produced between 1914 and 1925. At its peak, the mine was producing 40 tons of coal per day, but the average production was 10 tons per day. The first workings went down about 100 feet while the second workings reached a depth of 130 feet. There were six different operators during the period 1905 to 1914, which could account for the mine's low recovery rate. On June 6, 1919, the Bush Coal Company had as partners P. Thomson, Charles Laderoute, Kenneth Campbell and Harry Southgate.

Old Bush Mine, Date Uncertain

Provincial Archives of Alberta, Ernest Brown Collection B.1541A

Fire was discovered in the mine in March 1922 and sealed off. The fire again broke out in December 1923 under present day 30th Street and 108th Avenue and was apparently again sealed. Mining in the No. 2 workings ceased on March 27, 1925.

Bush (Davidson) Mine

Bush (Davidson) Mine, circa 1930

Photo courtesy
Doris Gibbs and the
Davidson Family

1917 to 1944. Mine No. 707. Location: River Lots 38 and 40. Entrances west of 36th Street and south of 104th Avenue. Recorded production (27 years of 28; no production 1919): 705,246 tons. Estimated average recovery: 57.5 per cent. Estimated average thickness of coal mined: 4 feet 9 inches.

Using his mineral rights in Beverly and along the river bank that had been purchased along with the property in 1912, Adam James (A.J.) Davidson started a coal mining operation which he registered in 1917 as the Beverly Coal and Gravel Company Limited #707. The first entrance, just above the North Saskatchewan river bed, was a drift mine cut into the bank in October 1917. The mine operated four months, produced 1,365 tons and shut down.

It reopened in the fall of 1920 and by February 1921 the mine inspector reported seven drifts into the bank of the river about 80 feet apart but only one drift is shown on the maps of the operation. A steam-powered engine pulled the coal cars along a long cable upslope from the river where the coal was graded on screens. On the top of the bank, Davidson and crew built a barn to house the mine horses and an engine room. A chute was installed at the top of the bank and another at the river and coal was sold on the valley rim in the spring and fall and down at the river in the winter. During the busy winter season, coal was also hauled to customers in Beverly and Edmonton by horse-drawn coal sleighs.

Bush (Davidson) Mine car, 1927

Photo courtesy Doris Gibbs and the Davidson Family

Considerable coal was produced from this drift mine in 1921/22 and in 1923, a hoisting shaft was installed at the rim of the bank at about 103rd Avenue and

36th Street. A tipple was constructed and fitted with screens for grading the coal and with chutes to transfer the coal into waiting trucks. An office building, weigh scales and a bunkhouse were constructed, along with a boiler room which housed the steam engine and steam boiler, electric hoist and provided

storage space for tools and the black smithing equipment. Hot water was piped from the steam boiler to the wash house, where miners took their showers.

In the mine's early days, A.J. had trouble keeping miners. After they were paid, they just disappeared and so, to combat the high turnover, he asked his daughter Cora if she would feed the miners. Cora agreed and soon had her hands full feeding miners, looking after her four small children and trying to keep a mine house clean and presentable. "It was very hard on my mother," says Doris Wilson Gibbs. "She was up early and worked long days." In 1928, A.J. leased the mine to Bush Mines Limited and he went on to start a dairy farm.

Bush Coal miners, January 10, 1937

City of Edmonton Archives, EA-160-1490

Bush Coal Company Ltd. trucks, 1940

City of Edmonton Archives, EA-160-245

By 1938, 100 foot and 200 foot longwall faces were operating, but it is not known precisely when the longwall system was introduced or when it was discontinued. When the mine was abandoned March 3rd, 1944, the area became a large gravel pit and that lowered and altered the shape of the land.

All the old buildings are long gone and modern houses now sit where the mine and farm used to be.

The Beverly Coal Mine

1931 to 1951. Mine No. 1366. Entrance east of 43rd Street and south of 121st Avenue. Recorded production (21 years of 21): 836,882 tons. Underground production: 817,000 tons. Recovery: 57.5 per cent. Estimated average thickness of underground coal mined: 5 feet.

Beverly Coal Mine miners, early 1930s

Photo courtesy
Zenobia Rockwell

In the depths of the Great Depression the Beverly Coal Mine was held up as a way to support and provide employment for local out-of-work coal miners and, for a time, it did just that. The mine was started in 1931 as a cooperative under municipal sponsorship, led by the town's secretary-treasurer Percy J. Rowe, grocer Alex Lastiwka and laundryman W.T. Walker. Rowe became general manager of the mine venture. The thinking was that the town could realize royalties through the sale of coal and, in so doing, help alleviate its economic crisis.

The town bought the coal rights within its boundaries and the cooperative began selling 500 shares at $100 each. The scheme held out the promise that, when the mine was making a profit, the shareholders would partake in the good fortune. The idea was intensely appealing to a populace tired of losing everything and soon about 90 per cent of the stakeholders were residents of Beverly.

Beginning of the Beverly Coal Mine, 1931

City of Edmonton Archives, EA-160-665

Work commenced sinking a shaft to the coal level 164 feet below the surface. A crew of workers descended upon the site near today's 43rd Street and 120th Avenue and, digging with shovels, they made slow but steady progress on a shaft measuring 36 feet by 14 feet. It was labourious, backbreaking work and, because of the dire economic situation, there was no money to buy timber for cribbing supports. Consequently, sidewalks in the town were ripped up and the boards bolted across 12 by 24 inch timbers transported from the Canadian National Railways yards by John Tymchuk and Mike Young. Dirt was hauled away by horse and wagon. The workers were paid in shares five dollars a week.

The shaft was finished in 1932 and was then divided into three vertical compartments - two with cages to transport men to the bottom of the shaft and then bring the coal up and the third with ladders in case of emergency. Oxygen to the miners was supplied by a shaft a half block east of the tipple and two enormous electric powered fans pushed the air through. Once the coal level had been reached, main tunnels measuring about 10 feet wide were dug. One tunnel went east just to 34th Street while another went west to 50th Street - the boundary between Beverly and the City of Edmonton. The tunnel going north of the main shaft was a short one. An underground river caused flooding in this tunnel, forcing its closure a short distance from the mine. The underground waterway wreaked havoc in the west tunnel workings as well. The south tunnel stretched from the west shaft to about 114th Avenue.

While the main tunnels were being opened, a tipple, 110 feet high, was built atop the main shaft. Machinery was needed but there was no money and so, in 1932 E.I. Clarke lent the mine $14,000 on demand notes meaning that, at any time, he could "demand" it back.

Beverly Mine Tipple, 1932

City of Edmonton Archives, EA-160-505

The seam of coal was six to six and a half feet deep and above the seam was a one foot thick layer of bone, with another 18 inch layer of coal above that. As the miners removed the six foot layer of coal, they removed the layer of bone but left intact the top layer of coal and that provided a ceiling which did not need to be braced. Off the main tunnel, men working in pairs removed coal in rooms, gradually enlarging them to about 75 feet wide. About 30 feet of coal was left between the rooms for support.

To remove the coal, a cutting machine like a big chain saw was used. At the base of the wall of coal, the cutter would carve out six to eight inches of coal and then small charges of dynamite were placed at the four corners of the wall. When the dynamite exploded, the wall of coal would tumble down the six to eight inches the cutting machine had removed. The men then loaded the coal on cars which ran on steel tracks. A man driving a single horse would pull two loaded cars at a time to a grouping place and, when there were about 20 cars in a group, a spike team of three horses, hitched single file, would pull the cars loaded with 2,500 to 2,800 pounds of coal to a parting - a meeting of two sets of tracks. Mike Young drove the spike horses for 11 years, with Rosie as his lead horse. He was paid $36 every two weeks for working a 14-hour a day shift. Coal sold for $4.50 a ton, delivered.

A main rope from the tipple brought 40 empty cars out to the parting, while a tail rope was hooked onto the full cars and hauled them back to the tipple. The power needed to control the main and tail ropes and shaft was supplied by a coal-fired steam boiler. Water for the boiler was hauled three barrels at a time from Goldby's well and, at night, 20 barrels were transported. Before the outbreak of the Second World War, there was one spike team, five single horses and ten to 12 horses in training at all times when the mine operated through the winters. The horses were brought up and pastured all summer. But then, after the start of the war, coal was needed year round and so the mine operated continuously and the horses were rotated into duty.

The coal cars were pushed into cages which were hauled up the tipple and the coal was weighed and stored. It was then put on shaker screens for grading depending on size. Varieties included larger lump coal, mine run coal (a mix of lump and small coal), five to six inch diameter stove coal, two inch diameter nut coal (which burned the hottest), one-inch stoker coal and slack, the remaining bits and dust. Coal trucks backed up to the chute of the type of coal they wanted and were loaded by opening a door at the end of the chute. As the coal was mined far underground, residents were often jolted awake by the blasting. "Boom, you'd feel it, windows and dishes would rattle, and you knew they were at it again," recalls long time resident Jennie Bodnar.

The sale of coal was good, but the company itself was not in good shape. In 1933, the Beverly Coal Mine claimed bankruptcy, leaving shareholders penniless and potentially throwing 120 men out of work. It took months for the McGillivray Royal Commission to sort out the mess and the outcome wasn't pleasant. Miners lost up to $70,000 in wages and businessmen were left with valueless stock. Assets estimated at $171,600 were turned over to E.I. Clarke, who held the demand note, and for $30,000 cash he assumed control of the mine. Clarke and his brother Jean operated it until the late 1940s when H. Davidson entered the picture and bought the mine and Davidson began operating it as the Beverly Coal Company Limited, with A.V. Carlson and Thomas Hays as partners.

Beverly Coal Company Ltd. trucks, 1937

City of Edmonton Archives, EA-160-218

Beverly Coal Mine, 1932

Glenbow Archives, Calgary, Canada ND-3-6219c

For a time, longwall mining was tried, but it proved too dangerous and not profitable. The longwall method may also have been responsible for triggering subsidence at the surface along 44th Street between 114th and 116th Avenues. With the market for coal softening and coal mines closing, the mine ceased pulling coal from the ground in 1951 and concluded operations awash in a trail of red link in March 1954, bringing to an end Beverly's coal mining days.

Other mines operating in Beverly included:

BUSH'S MINE

1901 to 1907. Mines No. 51 and 123. Location: River Lot 42, southeast of modern day 116th Avenue and 30th Street. Recorded production (four years of seven): 13,957 tons. Recovery: 25 per cent. Estimated average thickness of coal mined: 5 feet 6 inches.

BOOTH MINE

1924 to 1942. Mine No. 1167. Location: Under modern day Yellowhead Trail just west of the Beverly Bridge. Recorded production (19 years of 19): 30,973 tons. Recovery: 57.5 per cent. Estimated average thickness of coal mined: 3 feet 6 inches.

Several large mines also operated on the east side of the river. These operations employed many Beverly men, who walked across the railway bridge to work every day. The mines included the mammoth Black Diamond Mine, Fraser-Mackay Collieries and Marcus Collieries and the smaller Ottewell (Clover Bar) Mine, Blue Ribbon Mine, Stewart (Western) Mine and Daly Mine.

The Beverly Spur Tracks

Two spur lines ran south off the Grand Trunk Pacific/Canadian National Railways main line into Beverly. Newspaper reports indicate the easternmost spur to the Humberstone and Clover Bar Mines was completed in 1910. Land for the spur was transferred from Robertson-Davidson Limited to William Humberstone on August 4, 1917. Research by railway historian Alan Vanterpool reveals that in the September 1930 CNR Employee Timetable, this line was called the Humberstone Spur and was 73 car lengths long, which would make it at least 2,920 feet or little over a half mile. It went due south along the Government Road Allowance which parallels 34th Street, veered to the southeast, curved again to the south and then terminated.

The exact role of the westernmost spur is more uncertain. A 1921 CNR Employee Timetable notes that the spur was just east of the Edmonton Rail Yard Limit but the 1927 timetable only refers to the Humberstone Spur. It's not clear exactly when these lines ceased to be used, but the Humberstone Mine closed in 1934 and neither spur is listed in the 1940 employee timetable. There are indications the tracks were removed from the spurs sometime during the Second World War.

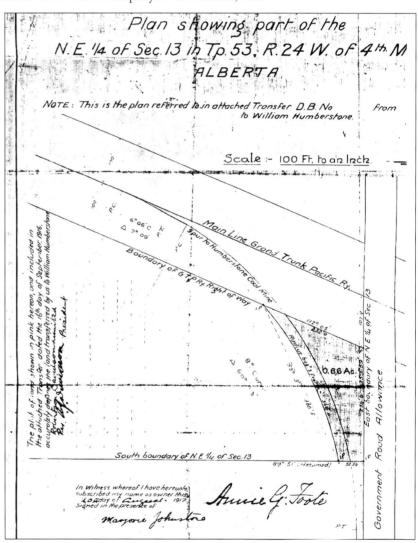

*Humberstone Railway
Spur Plan*

Artifact courtesy
Walter MacDonald

May Day Parade,
May 1, 1937

The Depression &
Second World War Years

Fehr Family in Edmonton, June 28, 1934

When the New York Stock Market crashed October 19, 1929, it sent shock waves around the world, triggering a global economic depression. By 1931, as many as 14,000 Edmontonians were supported by direct government relief - a ratio of about 17 per cent. With its coal and meat packing economy directly tied to production and manufacturing - sectors hit hard by falling commodity prices - Beverly took the force of the economic collapse even harder. In 1931, coal miners made 50 cents a day and worked a 14 hour shift but by the following year, more than a third of the town's workforce was out of work. A provincial study revealed that by the end of the 1930s, many Beverly families had been on welfare more than ten years.

It had been a slow and painful slide into the economic gutter for a community that started with so much promise back barely 20 years earlier. From an assessment topping $3 million in 1913, Beverly's appraised land value dropped

*Beverly Coal Mine,
1932*

Glenbow Archives,
Calgary, Canada
ND-3-6219b

to $756,200 in 1922 and further declined to $326,209 in 1932. Endeavouring to turn the fortunes around, town council jumped at an opportunity to gain some royalties from the sale of coal and provide employment for its poverty-stricken populace.

That was the genesis of the Beverly Coal Mine.

The Birth and Fall of Beverly Limited

Beverly Limited was formed in 1931 as a cooperative under municipal sponsorship. At a special meeting July 17, 1931, councillors voted to accept an offer from Beverly Limited to mine the coal owned by the town for 35 cents a ton and a minimum royalty payable on five tons within the first fiscal year. But Beverly Limited led a troubled existence right from the beginning. To finance the venture, the town borrowed money from the province, but those funds were soon exhausted and so the municipality paid wages in the form of vouchers redeemable at local stores. But store owners were leery of these vouchers and one storekeeper, called Mitchell, said that he would "paper his parlour" with the certificates, such was their value.

By October 1932, there were rumblings about the relationship between the municipality and the mine itself. At the October 31, 1932 council meeting, Mayor Percy B. Lawton offered that it would be "desirable to clean up the very ardent confusion and misunderstanding in the minds of the citizens regarding the status of the mine in the town." He suggested that a meeting be arranged at an early date so council members could confer with mine officials on such matters as the construction of the well ditch, royalties and graveling of roads. At a public meeting in December, the town's secretary-treasurer, Percy J. Rowe - who also served as general manager of the mine - was forced to explain the relationship between the Town and the Beverly Mine. "Since last year, the mine has been indirectly responsible for cutting the names of 50 families off the relief lists by giving them employment," Rowe told the gathering. "There is nothing unsafe or unsound in its present status. I have swept away all kinds of red tape and technicalities in fighting for the life of this mine but I have done so because I think the welfare and rights of the people come before such things." A rousing ovation greeted him at the end of his address. Just two months later, Rowe resigned his position as the Town's secretary-treasurer so he could "devote his entire time to the shareholders of Beverly Limited."

But, into the dark days of the Depression, ominous signs continued to mount, showing that the mine was in deep financial trouble. When Beverly Limited declared bankruptcy in early 1933, 120 jobs were thrown to the wind and shareholders were threatened with zero return on their investment. E.I. Clarke, who held a $14,000 demand note and took control of his troubled asset, appeared before council April 5,

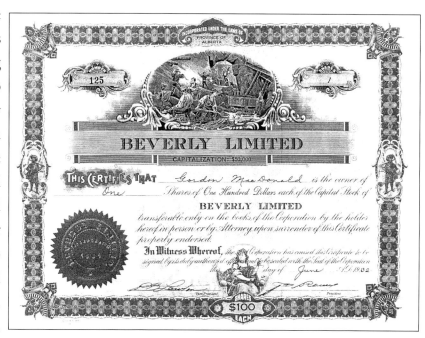

Beverly Limited Shares, 1932

Artifact courtesy
Walter MacDonald

1933 and asked that the royalties be reduced from 25 cents a ton to 15 cent a ton over the next four or five years and that wage holders, creditors and shareholders forego their claims for one year from May 1, 1933. Council resisted and so the mine stayed in limbo for many more weeks, the workforce uncertain, the town agitated by the turn of events.

On May 2, 1933 a special meeting of council heard from men contending discrimination in the mine and refuting the allegation they are "agitators to the detriment of the mine in the community." The unrest swelled, the RCMP intervened and the situation threatened to get even uglier. Two days later, Clarke offered another reorganization package, this one with workers to get one-quarter of their claims and creditors to get 3rd or 4th preferred stock. But Clarke refused to commit to employing Beverly men or instituting a fair wage clause. More negotiations followed in the days to come and eventually the town got 15 cents a ton, payable in cash, and the mine agreed that at least 60 per cent of the workforce would be men from Beverly, provided they had been resident in the community for a minimum of one year.

Caring and Compassion

In the depths of the Depression, with hundreds of Beverly residents out of

Beverly Coal Mine under construction

City of Edmonton Archives, EA-160-823

work and with no visible means of support, local churches and merchants dug in to help out. Typical of the generosity of the time was that shown by United Church Minister Rev. J.T. Stephens, who sought funds and clothing to assist those in dire need and, on many occasions, emptied his own pantry to feed those without food.

William Curtis recalled in a 1970 letter the time he and Rev. Stephens discovered a widowed mother of four children with no food in the house, no coal for the stove, and no stockings or shoes for the children. Curtis, Rev. Stephens and his wife rushed to All People's Mission to gather up whatever clothes and shoes that would fit and, while Mrs. Stephens stayed with the family, the two men went down to the Bush Mine to gather up waste coal. "We were caught by Frank Glossop, the night watchman," Curtis wrote. "We explained the circumstances and Frank jumped, also finding a few bags which were filled with good coal and with him we went back to the home. Frank reported the situation to his boss and the Bush Mine supplied coal to the family all winter, free."

The Province Steps In

The year was 1936, the Depression had stretched more than six years and Beverly's finances were in shambles. When the Town defaulted on its debentures, the Board of Utilities had taken control of the municipality's revenue. With practically no income, the town was just piling up more debt, issuing more relief slips to its needy citizens, vouching for school services it couldn't afford. The Alberta government prepared to step in and assume control. An emergency meeting of town council produced the following resolution: "Resolved that we vigorously protest the arbitrary and unwarranted action of the Provincial Government in invading the time honoured rights of Municipal self government by the notification of the impending appointment of an Administrator."

Indignation notwithstanding, the province agreed to give the town one more year to get its finances in order. Acting on legal advice, council pushed ahead to sue the Beverly Limited Mine for $30,000 for breach of contract. But the town lost the suit and, with court costs added to the equation, the total cost was $6,299 - and that broke the town. The town's deficit jumped from $27,244.36 in 1936 to $31,244.92 in 1937.

The council, defiant right to the end, passed a motion at their penultimate meeting January 29, 1937 requesting the province to "declare a three or four-year moratorium on all interest and public debts. This would enable the

Beverly Town Council, circa 1934

City of Edmonton Archives, EA-160-335

municipality to get on their feet. Unlike the present arrangement the taxpayers of Beverly are compelled to meet a 50-year debenture debt which, when paid, would amount to three times the original debt. This makes it utterly impossible for the taxpayers to meet their obligations."

The plea apparently had no impact as, just a few days later, Nicholas Rushton, the Assistant Deputy Minister of Municipal Affairs, was appointed the town's administrator. He assumed the helm February 17, 1937. "Good morning, gentlemen. I am the new administrator," the record shows Rushton greeting council that historic day. "Please hand over the books, cash and accounts." The ousted council was comprised of Mayor Frank Wagner and Councillors Dompe, Doolan, Floden, Gerry, Kopiak and Thompson, with T.B. Major as Secretary. A royal commission into the town's affairs was launched, amidst allegations of misappropriated funds. However, those allegations were never proven in court.

The wrangling over the town's affairs shone the spotlight on municipal governance and, in 1938, the Beverly Electors Association was formed to protect citizens' rights. As the Town hobbled along under the watchful eye of the provincial "Big Brother," work at the one remaining mine and the nearby packing Plants - Swifts, Burns, Canada Packers - also helped cash-strapped residents put food on the table. But still there just wasn't enough work to go around and many families packed up and left. Between 1931 and 1941, Beverly's population as tabulated by the Dominion Census, tumbled from 1,111 to 981.

Beverly Gravel Plant, 1936

City of Edmonton Archives, EA-160-1547

By the end of the 1930s, the town, under the administrator, was reported to be "living within its income." When the Second World War broke out, many Beverly citizens volunteered to serve, as they had in the Great War nearly 25 years earlier. This time, the price paid was not quite so dear; five Beverly residents died from injuries suffered during WWII.

The hope that washed across the country in the days after the war was soon to be felt in Beverly. For a coal mining town that had lost its mines, struggled without an industrial base and endured a lack of modern services, the best was yet to come.

McGavin's Bread man, 1932

City of Edmonton
Archives, EA-160-1451

Beverly School, 1952

Photo courtesy
Honore Dahlberg West

Places of Worship and Learning

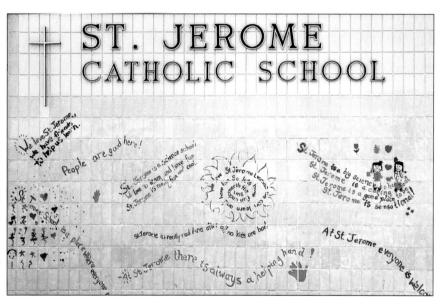

St. Jerome Catholic School, May 2000

Early schools and churches in Beverly were much more than places of learning and worship. In the days before community leagues, municipal halls or hotels with meeting rooms, they were focal points in the town - places where people gathered for celebration and veneration. They were the heart of the community's social and spiritual development, a place for neighbours to come together in a spirit of fellowship and for children to be nurtured and to grow. Because residents didn't often leave town and recreation and cultural diversions were few and far between, a special event at a local church or a student assembly at the school was important.

The Beverly school system began as the Edmonton Highlands School District No. 2292, formed in 1910. On Saturday, March 29th, 1913, the first Beverly meeting of the school board was held at the store of F.M. Hayes on Alberta Avenue. Robert Walker, the chairman of the Village of Beverly, served as chair. At that meeting, after briefly considering the name Beacon Heights School District, the title was officially changed to Beverly School District No. 2292.

The Beverly Central School

117th Avenue and 38th Street. Opened 1913, demolished 1955. Named for town.

One of the first orders of business of the new Board was the construction of a school. Duke MacRolling, a local builder, was commissioned to draw plans for a four-room schoolhouse. MacRolling also served as building commissioner for the school, which was constructed in about three months and opened in September 1913. The Beverly Central School quickly became the most well known and used gathering place in the fledgling community.

Beverly Central School, 1932

City of Edmonton Archives, EA-160-502

The two-storey building, with four classrooms, was wood framed and faced with brick. There was no electricity and heat was provided by a coal and wood fired boiler system in the basement that sometimes couldn't cope with the bitterly cold winters. City water was delivered by water truck and pumped into a cistern in the basement for the school's water supply. This tiny schoolhouse, out in the middle of a windswept field southeast of the modern day Drake Hotel, was a place of learning for thousands of local children from Grade One through Grade Eight over the next 40 years. Beverly students went to Highlands Junior High for Grade Nine and their choice of Eastwood or Victoria Composite High for Grades 10 through 12.

Stories of life at Beverly Central are legendary. Because there was no electricity, school ended earlier during the winter months. If it was a windy winter day, the boiler could not keep up and, if the school got too cold, students were sent home early. By September 1950, the old school house was literally tumbling down. The brick veneer on the exterior began crumbling, forcing a four-day holiday for the school's 136 pupils. Engineers of the department of public works found what the Edmonton Bulletin called the "tumbledown old schoolhouse" unsafe when they tested the structure September 16th and pushed a section of brick veneer from the exterior wall out into the school yard.

The rest of the brick veneer was peeled off and, in its place, four by eight foot sheets of black ten test cladding became the facade. That's how the venerable structure, in its last years of life, came to be known as the "Old Black School." Its 40-year life at an end, the school was demolished in 1955 by Adby Construction. The schoolyard of R.J. Scott Elementary now occupies part of the original site. Ironically, title searches conducted by the school district in 1955 revealed that much of the land of the Beverly Central School site had not been registered in the name of the Beverly School District back at its beginnings but had remained in the name of the previous owner.

Farquhar School

North of 121st Avenue between 45th and 46th Streets. Opened December 1915 and closed June 1918. It was named for Colonel Farquhar of the Princess Patricia Regiment, who died in action during the early days of WWI.

When the Beverly School District decided to build a second school, trustees selected a location that had been considered but rejected for

Beverly Cenotaph and Central School, 1933

City of Edmonton Archives
EA-160-1168

the first school because the site was too far north and too wet. They hired Ernest W. Morehouse to design a school that, as renderings show, featured some of the renowned architect's classic Georgian Revival flourish. Morehouse, who was one of the best known architects in the formative years of The Highlands neighbourhood, also drew the plans for the mansions of Magrath and Holgate, the Ash Residence and the Highlands Methodist Church as well as many commercial blocks.

Trustees considered naming the new school after postmaster Thomas Dando but settled on Colonel Farquhar, who died in action during the early days of the First World War. The high water table created problems right from the beginning for contractor H. Valk and his construction crew. Even before the school was officially opened with a concert and dance Monday, December

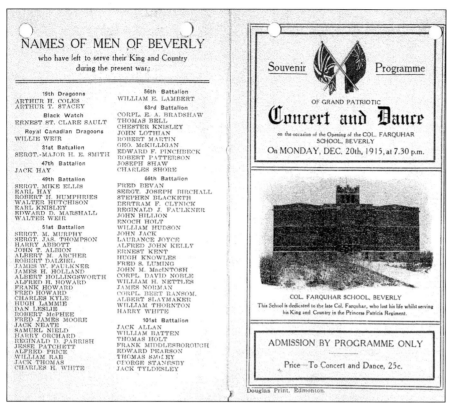

*Programme of Farquhar
School Opening, 1915*

Artifact courtesy
Honore Dahlberg West

20th, 1915, water was entering the basement through holes in the foundation walls. Plaster was falling from the walls and ceilings and window ledges were coming apart.

At the school board's meeting of August 8th, 1916, a motion was passed which authorized caretaker John Abbott to "secure such help as is needed to perform the work of draining the basement and cleaning out and widening the ditch of the Col. Farquhar School." The work didn't solve the problem and, as water continued to play havoc with the foundation, the bills for repair work kept mounting.

Faced with cash flow problems, the trustees voted to close the school in June 1918. It sat empty for several years and repeated attempts to sell it were unsuccessful. Finally in 1928, the building was sold as salvage for a paltry $1,300. The total loss to ratepayers was more than $25,000.

Percy Benjamin Lawton

Percy Benjamin Lawton, or P.B. as he was known, was Beverly's longest serving and best loved teacher and principal. Lawton began teaching in Beverly in 1927 and reached the position of Supervisor of Beverly Schools before retiring in 1957, a remarkable 30 year record of service in the same jurisdiction. During that time, he taught 805 students.

Lawton was born in Lacombe in 1902 and came to Edmonton in 1905. He was educated at Queen Alexandra School and Strathcona Collegiate Institute and began his teaching career at Duffield, west of Edmonton, in 1922. He taught there for two years before moving to Angle Lake for a one year stint. And then Lawton came to Beverly in 1927.

While other teachers in early Beverly used their position as stepping stone to other opportunities, Lawton reflected that, "as soon as I arrived in Beverly, it seemed like home." When Lawton first arrived, it was common to hear the town's children referred to in city schools as "Beverly Bums," but Lawton helped change that by instilling a strong work ethic, a motivation to learn and a atmosphere that helped give the town a good reputation for education.

Over the years, stories involving the teacher and principal became the stuff of legend. Lawton's old Essex automobile was the butt of many pranks, including one involving yet to be Edmonton Mayor William Hawrelak. It seems Hawrelak and four other students were caught trying to push the Essex out of the school yard. The five were dispatched to the bush to each select a sturdy willow switch. Hawrelak found a good stocky one, while the others, anticipating what was coming, chose slender twigs. The story goes that Lawton used the sturdy cane on the four who thought they could outsmart the principal and released the future mayor with a stern warning.

Percy Benjamin Lawton

Photo courtesy Stella Skrzekowski

Another time, Lawton reprimanded a group of boys who had carried the school's outhouse up onto the front steps. He knew who did it and made them pick it up and haul it back over its rightful hole, with the instigator at the appropriate place to catch the aroma of the deed. Mr. Lawton, who was sometimes endearingly called "baldy" by his students, also found time for public affairs and served as a town councillor in 1931 and was elected mayor of Beverly the following year.

Lawton was a long time resident of 4823 Ada Boulevard, a house near the North Saskatchewan River. In his years of service, he helped the Beverly school system grow from a single four-room school to a modern $2 million system with classrooms for 1,500 students. At a ceremony commemorating his 30 years of service to the community in 1957, he was given a plaque which read: "Presented to P.B. Lawton for outstanding service to school and community, 1927 to 1957, from the Town of Beverly." Former colleague Harold Gerry, master of ceremonies for the event, noted that not only did Lawton "lay the foundation of citizenship in this town, but he paddled the foundation of many of the leading citizens and many of them are here tonight to thank him for it."

Percy Benjamin Lawton, 1940

Photo courtesy
Phyllis (Hnidan) Bonke

Even though he was suffering from cancer, Lawton remained at his job as superintendent until the month before he died. Lawton died January 2nd , 1962, at the age of 59 and was buried at Mount Pleasant Cemetery. In a letter to the Edmonton Journal published January 15, two weeks after Lawton's death, long time associate George Pojalow called him one of the greatest human beings who ever lived. "During the depression years, as Mayor of the Town of Beverly, Mr. Lawton was a true champion of Beverly and its populace, never thinking of himself, working ceaselessly for the town, school and his pupils whom he deeply loved, with no compensation for his efforts. If any of the children needed clothing, Mr. Lawton came up with his best efforts and we received them." Pojalow noted that Lawton had the esteem of old and young, rich and poor. "If there was a heaven above, Mr. Lawton is right up front there, as he was in Beverly."

The "H" Central School

Between 116th Avenue and 117th Avenue and 38th Street and 40th Street. Opened May 1st , 1950. Named after the old school on the site.

Named for its design configuration, which resembled a capital "H," this six-room schoolhouse was built to help alleviate overcrowding and to eventually replace the Beverly Central School. At its official opening May 1st, 1950, the $60,000 school was touted as the first school in western Canada to use all steel plating for exterior walls and roofing. The new facility soon came to be nicknamed "the tin school." Designed by Fred H. MacDonald, the school was financed through the issue of $140,000 worth of debentures.

This modern school with a water system, indoor plumbing, drinking fountains and flush toilets (but no hookup to municipal water) created a stir in the community. Many of the young students, who didn't have indoor plumbing at home, needed to learn how to use the toilets. Nearly 500 people turned out for the official opening - citizens, school children, government and school officials from local jurisdictions and others in Rocky Mountain House, Lacombe, Red Deer and Olds school divisions. The ribbon signifying the official opening was cut by Ivan Casey, Minister of Education.

The school, with its six classrooms, library, playroom and teachers' offices, was built to accommodate 310 students. But R.S. Sheppard, superintendent of Edmonton Public Schools, prophesied correctly when he told the gathering that the new facility likely wouldn't be big enough. "I have no doubt that almost before the building is completed and occupied, you will wish that it had been built larger," he told the audience. Quoting recent vital statistics on school populations Mr. Sheppard said that "by 1953 there will be an increase of 600,000 children in elementary grades in Canada," a one-third increase to what were, in 1950, record enrollments. Like the Colonel Farquhar School so many years earlier, the new Central School experienced that sinking feeling from bad soil conditions and it was demolished sometime after 1962.

CUTTING RIBBON to open one of finest schools in Canada is Alberta's minister of education, Ivan Casey, who was on hand to officially open new Beverly school yesterday.

Beverly Gets Canada's Most Modern School

Beverly officially opened its new all-steel construction school—first of its kind in western Canada—yesterday afternoon and just about everybody in town was on hand for the long awaited ceremony.

It was the first such ceremony in the town since 1915 when its original — and only — four-room brick schoolhouse was opened.

Unmindful of the dust stirred up from the new school grounds, prominent provincial government, city and school board officials shared opening ceremonies with Beverly school musicians.

LARGE ASSEMBLAGE

Large assemblage of parents, students, and teachers were on hand to hear official speeches and to inspect "our" new school's modern fixtures and appointments after Hon. Ivan Casey cut the broad green ribbon across the school doors.

For a "good luck omen" he cut the ribbon with his left hand—the hand nearest the heart—which apparently describes the way the department feels about Beverly's new $80,000, six-room schoolhouse.

Besides the minister, speakers included R. S. Sheppard, superintendent of Edmonton public schools, Beverly's Mayor Albert Hairsine, Mrs. Edna Evans, chairman of the Beverly School Board, and Dr. Lou Heard, Social Credit MLA, Edmonton.

ON DOUBLE SHIFT

Some of the town's 280 pupils have been accommodated in Edmonton schools while two grades have been on double shift in the Beverly United Church. Others have been on double shift in school proper.

Mr. Sheppard told the gathering that no sooner would the new school be filled than the new would be felt for another.

He said he had one piece of advice: "Get a good home-school association going."

The minister of education called the new school "a pioneer in type," adding, "it should give pupils just a little more incentive to well."

The new school will have three classrooms in use almost immediately, Principal P. B. Lawton announced.

Designed on the "H" plan the classrooms, library, play room and teachers' offices will provide facilities for 310 pupils.

Beacon Heights School

4610 121 Avenue. Officially opened November 13th , 1953. Named for the district of Beacon Heights.

Overwhelmed by the hundreds of new students pouring into the district every year in the early 1950s, the school board passed Bylaw No. 5 on March 14th , 1952, which authorized borrowing $306,372 for new school site and erection of a new building. The money was used to build the six classroom Beacon Heights School, which was officially opened Friday, November 13th, 1953.

More than 300 people turned out for the opening ceremonies, where supervising principal P.B. Lawton called the school the first step towards a new system of schools for the town. "When the Beverly Heights school, south of 118th Avenue on 47th Street is completed, the children in the lower grades will not have to cross the busy 118th Avenue on their way to school," he said.

Enrollment at the new Beacon Heights School was 240 - more than a third of the total of 625 children in the four Beverly schools. The opening of Beacon Heights brought the number of classrooms in the district to 18 - equal to Beverly's number of instructors. But perhaps the most welcome feature of the new facility was its water and sewer installations - which were a first for a Beverly school. Running water was made possible when the City of Edmonton permitted connections to city mains three-and-a-half blocks from the school.

Designed by Patrick Campbell-Hope and Associates, the building was put together by R. Vollan Construction. Its total cost was $126,000 - $4,000 under budget. A story in the November 14th , 1953 edition of the Edmonton Journal reported that the six rooms with 11 foot ceilings "are well lighted with large windows and semi-indirect lights...modern desks...specially treated green blackboards" and the floors are "covered with linoleum in a variety of soothing colors." A well-equipped library and 70 foot long playroom rounded out the school's facilities. The first principal was William Nekolaichuk.

A five-classroom addition and gymnasium was added in 1960. The $102,450 expansion was built by Platten Bros. Construction. A 1967

Beacon Heights School, May 2000

assessment by the Edmonton Public School Board found the school to be in poor physical condition - a quick 14 year deterioration. In a May 16, 1967 story in the Edmonton Journal, Principal John Sywolos noted two-storey frame schools like Beacon Heights were often built quickly in the early 1950s and Beverly, feeling the crunch brought on by spiraling student numbers, did the "best they could dollar for dollar."

Beacon Heights School, May 2000

Beverly Heights School

47th Street and 115th Avenue. Opened January 28, 1955. Named for the district of Beverly Heights.

Using the design from Beacon Heights School, the Beverly School District authorized the construction of Beverly Heights School in 1954. The opening of the school in early 1955 at long last took the load off that the Beverly Central School - now on the verge of demolition - had been carrying for more than 40 years. With Percy Benjamin Lawton as chairman and a dedication from Hon. A. Aalborg, Minister of Education, Beverly Heights School was officially opened January 28th, 1955. It was the first time the provincial Minister of Education had proclaimed a Beverly school open and the significance of the event was noted by Mayor Charles Floden.

Constructed for $125,000, the eight-classroom school was quickly filled as young families poured into Beverly. But, as the children aged and fewer new families moved into the district in the late 1960s, enrollment began to decline. The school's lack of gymnasium and library proved to be detrimental in the eyes of the Edmonton Public School Board and by 1971 the Board was proposing to close the school and shift students to nearby R.J. Scott and Mount Royal schools. Opposition from parents and community groups managed to stall that plan for a time. But by September 1980, enrolment had tumbled to fewer than 50 students and only two of the school's eight classrooms were in use and the inevitable followed. A decision was made to close the school.

The Province takes over the Beverly Public School Board

As the province had done when the town's finances fell apart in the 1930s, it stepped in and took control of the Beverly School Board in 1955. R.J. Scott was appointed official trustee by the Alberta government when the board was unable to meet the schools' financial responsibilities. Scott held the position until October 27th, 1960 when the six schools were returned to the jurisdiction of the public school board. The half dozen schools at the time taught 1,571 students and employed 56 teachers.

Beverly Separate School District Number 52

The idea of establishing a Separate School District for Beverly had been raised at various times going back to the 1920s, but it wasn't until 1953 that the plan really took root at the urging of Rev. Henry Peet, the Catholic priest at St. Mary's Church. A survey of the Roman Catholic and Ukrainian Catholic parishioners found more than enough support. The issue went before Beverly ratepayers in 1955 and on September 1st the first Board meeting of the Beverly Separate School District Number 52 was convened. John Charuk, operator of the local Texaco "Strato Chief" service station on 118th Avenue and 38th Street, was named the first Chairman of the Board, with Jack Weber as secretary/treasurer and Frank Greschuk, Bill Knor, Stanley Maskwa, Fred Nash, Joseph Schell and Michael Tyrkalo as Board members. Weber, as secretary/treasurer, was the district's only paid staff member at the time.

St. Bernadette School

11917 40 Street. Officially opened March 25th, 1957.

Acclaimed for its hexagonal shape and individual heating in each of its 10-classrooms, the opening of St. Bernadette School generated great excitement in the community. At the official ceremony, W.E. Frame, the chief superintendent of schools for the provincial department of education, presented the keys to the school's first principal, Mrs. E. McNamee.

The Board hoped to have the school ready for September 1956, but the time line was just too tight and classes didn't begin until March 1957. In the meantime, the 140 grade one to nine students were taught at the Slovak National Hall on 118th Avenue at 46th Street. "That building was so old that the squeaky floors were distracting the students and teachers alike," Charuk recalls. "And so classes were moved to the temporary St. Mary's Church and that was the beginning of the true classroom concept."

Based on schools at Taber and Grande Prairie, Alberta, the design for St. Bernadette's featured a round floor plan with five-sided rooms for maximum light penetration, minimum hall space and no need for a basement. It was known as a Maxim-Lite school and was the brainchild of the Lethbridge architectural firm Fookes and Milne. Contractors were Southern Alberta Construction of Lethbridge, the company which also erected the Taber school.

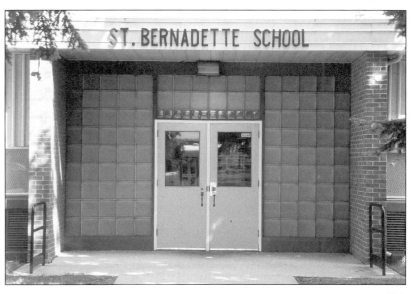

St. Bernadette School, May 2000

Built on a thrifty budget of $193,000 plus land costs, there wasn't enough money for adornments like a fancy sign and so, when a contractor wanted $25 a letter to make the sign in metal, long time Beverly resident Fred Nash came to the rescue, picking out plywood scraps from the construction site. He cut the letters with a fretsaw, sawed a broom handle into one-inch lengths for mounting studs and crafted the school's sign, which adorned the front entrance for many years.

Lawton Junior High School

11602 40 Street. Officially opened October 18th, 1957. Named for long time principal and school superintendent, Percy Benjamin Lawton.

The eight-classroom Lawton Junior High, a facility called "modern concrete and veneer" brought Grade Nine instruction to Beverly for the first time in its history. It was also designed by Patrick Campbell-Hope and Associates, the school district's favourite architectural firm of the 1950s. The facility featured a science lab, gymnasium, home economics, manual training (industrial arts) and typing room - features not previously combined under one roof in a Beverly school. The school greatly helped alleviate overcrowding, which had reached serious levels in 1956. But as more families poured into "booming

Lawton Jr. High School, May 2000

Beverly," the need continued to escalate and just three years after it opened, a nine-classroom addition, built by Walters Construction Limited, was completed at Lawton.

Ironically, it was Beverly's amalgamation with Edmonton that cost the town any chance of getting a high school. If citizens had voted against amalgamation, there are indications that plans to build a new high school would have proceeded to design stage.

R. J. Scott Elementary School

11610 38 Street. Officially opened March 24th, 1959. Named for inspector, teacher and trustee for Beverly Schools.

The 10-room R.J. Scott School, also designed by Patrick Campbell-Hope and Associates, was constructed in 1958 at a cost of $166,800. It was erected by Poole Construction and officially opened March 24th, 1959.

The school was named for R.J. Scott, inspector, teacher and trustee for Beverly schools. Scott began his teaching career in Ontario in 1908 and moved to Alberta in 1912 where he was principal of an Edmonton school. He graduated from the University of Alberta with a Bachelor of Arts degree in 1929 and that year was appointed inspector. Scott first worked in Beverly in 1939 when he was inspector of the Sturgeon School Division, which at the time included Beverly schools. He retired as a provincial school inspector in 1955 and was appointed official trustee of Beverly schools acting in place of the school board.

R.J. Scott Elementary Schoool, May 2000

Abbott School

12045 34 Street. Officially opened October 26th, 1960. Named for long time Beverly custodian, Abraham Abbott.

"Abbott School opened in style" read the headline in the Beverly Page as the Edmonton area's only school named for a custodian was officially unveiled. More than 300 residents crowded the auditorium to hear Percy Lawton, Superintendent of Beverly Schools, pay tribute to Abraham Abbott, who came to Beverly in 1912, served in the First World War and then became caretaker of Beverly Central School in 1922. It was a post he held until his retirement in 1959 - a remarkable 37 year record of service.

"During these 36 years, Mr. Abbott has been a faithful servant of the schools and a true friend of the children," Lawton told the gathering. "When I took the schools from Mr. Thomas long ago, I was told, in Mr. Abbott, you have a jewel of a man. He is the most honest and responsible individual I ever met. I have known him for 36 years and no truer words were said of anyone."

Lawton concluded his remarks by observing that, "Mr. Abbott didn't gamble, drink nor smoke with the result that he always had some money . . . to give away at the most crucial moment."

Abbott was born in Derbyshire, England in 1887 and left there in 1911, making the exodus to North America along with many other eager immigrants. He settled in Lashburn, Saskatchewan and then, in 1912, married and moved to Edmonton where the couple raised three children - Hedley, Dorothy and Clifford. For a time he worked for the City of Edmonton, until he joined the Canadian Army as part of the Canadian Expeditionary Force for service in World War One. He served overseas from 1914 to 1919 and sustained a leg injury that would be with him as a limp for the rest of his life. When he returned to civilian life, he became a custodian at the Beverly School. His son Clifford became a celebrated Second World War flier.

Mrs. Abbott died at an early age and Mr. Abbott went to live with his brother William and his sister-in-law at 4455 Ada Boulevard. Olivena Horne, a teacher at the school, fondly remembers him as an early riser. He usually walked from his home on Ada Boulevard to the school at 116th Avenue and 40th Street and she says he always went at the same time. "You could set your watch by him. He would stoke up the big black furnace with coal and get the school warm enough to house the students for the day."

Former students fondly recall "Captain," Mr. Abbott's faithful German Shepherd dog who went everywhere with him. After the Beverly Central School was closed, Abbott went to work at Beacon Heights and Beverly Heights Schools until his retirement March 20, 1959.

Abe Abbott, 1950

Photo courtesy
Jean Kaminsky Kozak

Abbott was active in the development of the Beverly Methodist Church and, in its early days, he and William Curtis, another long time resident, would erect the tent for services each Sunday. During the Depression years, Abbott helped build the United Church on 38th Street, north of 118th Avenue. In the 40's the church was moved to 43rd Street and 118th Avenue. He remained active in the church, sang in the choir and served as a member of the church board from 1913 until his death in 1964 in British Columbia.

The school named in Abbott's honour was built on land east of 34th Street and north of 120th Avenue purchased from the Konopacki family in 1959 for $33,000. Designed by J. Gardiner of Patrick Campbell-Hope and Associates, construction commenced in December 1959 under the supervision of Whitham and Company contractors. The school was completed in August 1960 and readied for the start of the school year. Official opening was October 26, 1960.

Abbott School,
May 2000

St. Nicholas Separate Junior High

3643 115 Avenue. Officially opened December 4th , 1960.

Compared with the Beverly Roman Catholic School Division's round St. Bernadette School, St. Nicholas School was a more conventional rectangular design, but it was still noteworthy. It was designed by the teachers, with an entrance planned for accessibility and the noisy areas like the gym and the industrial arts shop physically separated from where quiet was needed.

Construction on the $357,222 building began in October 1959 and was completed in August 1960. The school featured 12-classrooms, home economics room, workshop, science room, library, typing room, medical room and gymnasium. Enrolment the year it opened was 200 students.

When St. Nicholas added Grade 12 to become at last a full fledged High School and offer classes in all 12 grades, the hopes of pioneering priest Father Peet had been realized. The last wish of the Beverly Roman Catholic School Division, when it turned over its assets to Edmonton for amalgamation in 1962, was that the high school would continue. It didn't and, to this day, Beverly students must leave the district for grades 10, 11 and 12. However, now students don't have to pay the $100 to $200 annual non-resident fee as they did until amalgamation.

St. Nicholas Separate Junior High, May 2000

The Roman Catholic School Division later opened two more elementary schools - St. Jerome at 3310 107th Avenue and St. Sophia at 3010 119th Avenue. St. Sophia was later sold and converted to use as the Abbottsfield Recreation Centre.

East Edmonton Christian School

36 Street and 117 Avenue. Opened 1955.

It was 1945 when a group of Christian parents formed a society with the aim of establishing Christian Day Schools where their children could be educated in accordance with their beliefs and convictions. Under the leadership of Rev. P. De Koekkoek, pastor of the First Christian Reformed Church, the Edmonton Society for Christian Education was founded. In the autumn of 1949 the Calvin Central Christian School began classes in the basement of the First Christian Reformed Church in Norwood. Initial enrolment was 21 pupils. Property was soon acquired at 102nd Street and 110th Avenue and, through donations of money and labour, a new school was built and opened in September 1951. Enrolment topped 80 students.

Faith Lutheran School, May 2000

Each successive year brought with it an increase in enrolment and, by the autumn of 1954, the maximum of 134 students had been reached and applications were being rejected. The young society purchased property at 36th Street and 115th Avenue and in the spring of 1955 a five-room facility, Calvin Christian School-East was constructed. It opened its doors in September and the enrolment of both schools reached 240 pupils.

While Canadian schools did little to mark the proclamation of the controversial new Canadian flag on February 15, 1965, the Calvin Christian

School held a ceremony which featured the lowering of the Red Ensign by grade six student Nick Spronk and the raising of the new Canadian maple leaf flag. Principal Peter S. Uitvlugt read the Proclamation and led an assembly of students around O Canada, the new national anthem. Parents and friends also joined in the ceremony, which was the only one held in the area. The school building was sold in February 1998 to the Faith Lutheran School and April 1st, 1998 became the Lutheran School Society.

Rundle Heights Elementary

11005 34th Street. Officially opened December 9th, 1966. Named after the Reverend Robert T. Rundle, Methodist missionary.

Students who attended the 12-room Rundle Heights School in its opening year were given the first opportunity to study and learn from the diary of Robert Rundle, the Wesleyan Missionary who, preaching as he worked his way west in 1840, arrived in Edmonton that autumn. He was the first resident missionary of any church in the area and was one of the first white men to speak out against the liquor trade, which was being used to sway First Nations peoples. During the week of the opening ceremonies, Principal D.C. Willows expressed the hope that his students would learn from Rundle the value of doing a job well, valuing certain principles and living by them. An addition and modifications to the school were completed in 1972.

Rundle Heights Elementary, May 2000

The Schools at Amalgamation

When Beverly merged with Edmonton December 30, 1961, the Beverly School system comprised 1,038 students and 40 teachers, while the Beverly Separate system had 491 students and 21 teachers. To prevent conflicts over salary, Beverly public schools adopted the Edmonton salary schedule in September 1961.

CHURCHES

Beverly Methodist and United Churches

The Methodist Church, one of the forerunners of the United Church, came to Beverly in 1912 when Rev. W.A. Lewis was appointed to direct a Central Edmonton Mission. From his base in North Edmonton he hauled around a large tent for worship services at several local districts, including Beverly. There are indications the big red and white Methodist tent was where the first meeting of Beverly Village Council was held. Early on, the Beverly Methodist Church was an outreach of All Peoples' Mission, which became the Bissell Centre. A variety of people provided ministerial leadership, including Reverends W.H. Pike, Ponich, Kenneth Kingston and Robert H. Leitch, who is listed as Pastor in 1914. That year, the membership list included 33 names. Women were very involved in the operation of the local church through the Women's Mission Society (W.M.S.).

Beverly United Church, circa 1955

Artifact courtesy Walter MacDonald

A building was constructed on 38th Street between 119th and 120th Avenues sometime between 1917 and 1925, a building that church leader William E. Curtis described as "a boxlike structure with a four-sided roof and a cubicle on top, very hard to heat, with badly cracked plaster walls." In the mid 1930s, under the guidance of Curtis and Rev. Dr. J.T. Stephens, effort began to find a bigger home for the church and the two men convinced Nicholas Rushton, the town's administrator, that vacant land along 118th Avenue at 43rd Street would be far better served as a playground with a church building adjacent from which the playground could be supervised. Rushton agreed and gave full title to the church for $1.00. Curtis later wrote it was a good thing because: "Reverend Stephens and I had exactly 50 cents each in our pockets! We handed it over at once sealing the deal."

With Bert Colby overseeing the work, the existing church was readied to be moved to the new location. "Adby Construction lifted the building onto dollies and the grand march down 118th Avenue (a dirt road) began with Vicky Jossul driving the tractor," Curtis recalled. "A new basement with concrete walls awaited; the building came to rest with Adby Construction discovering that there was no head room, however no changes could be made." To cover the broken plaster, Rev. Stephens asked the crew erecting the Kresge's Building on 101st Street and 101 A Avenue if the church could use the 3/4 inch plywood hoarding. They gave the entire four by eight foot sheets to the church and that's what was used to seal the inside of the structure.

Beverly United Church, 1976

Photo by H. A. Hollingworth, City of Edmonton Archives, EA-289-06

It was not until August 16th , 1956 that the first "full-time" minister, George A. Sauder, was appointed to Beverly. As thousands of newcomers flooded into Beverly during the boom of the 1950s, the old church became ever more cramped. By 1959, talk of the need for a new building began to circulate. In 1963, with the congregation faced with a cash crunch that never seemed to go away, the old church was sold. For two years, while funding for a new structure was being sought, plans were made and the new church erected at 11910 40 Street, the congregation met at Lawton Junior High School. Under the direction of Building Committee Chairman Vern Curtis (son of William), volunteers worked to complete the electrical, heating, plumbing and drywalling. The basement was ready for use in 1967 and the following year, the main floor was completed. A special dedication service was held April 28th, 1968 and the church has served the congregation since.

Beverly United Church, May 2000

The Anglican Church came to Beverly as early as 1913 and a place of worship named for St. James was apparently located on the east side of 38th Street near 119th Avenue. The church ceased operations sometime after 1915.

Beverly Presbyterian Church

East side of Beverly Boulevard (38th Street) at 117th Avenue. Operating 1914. Demolished 1958.

In its early days, the Beverly Presbyterian Church was guided by Rev. Frank D. Roxborough, who served 1914 to 1925. Rev. Roxborough was also in charge of North Edmonton and was the clerk of the Edmonton Presbyterian Presbytery from 1917 to 1925. He went on to be Moderator of the Alberta Synod in 1920-21 and Commissioner to General Assembly in 1917 and 1924. The building also served at various times as a two-room elementary school house for Beverly children and was demolished in 1958 by Adby Construction.

The Catholic Church in Beverly

Until 1916, Catholics living in Beverly celebrated their mass at private homes and by traveling to North Edmonton. On special Sundays, Beverly Catholics made pilgrimages to North Edmonton for Mass - first at the Swift's Packing Plant where worship was held by the Franciscan Fathers of the North Edmonton Monastery and later in a little chapel and then a larger church which was built near the monastery. In January 1915, Archbishop Emile Legal asked the Franciscan monks to oversee the Beverly mission and Rev. Father Martin Dietrich was placed in charge. On Sunday, January 31st , 1915 the first mass in Beverly was celebrated in a private home and local residences, including that of the Haverstock families, became the places of worship for the next year.

The following year, Rev. Father Ethelbert arrived from the east and

St. Paul Catholic Church, May 2000

began lending his help in districts overseen by the Franciscans. In Beverly, he built a tiny white church measuring 22 feet by 40 feet at 3635 116th Avenue. With a bell tower, brass bell and white exterior the church resembled old English Gothic architecture. The first service in the new church was given Sunday, March 19th, 1916 by Rev. Ethelbert and on that day a special choir from North Edmonton sang. The Edmonton Journal reported that, while small, the new church was very pretty and already a credit to Catholics in Beverly. Archbishop Legal blessed the new church on May 28th, 1916 and, according to the Franciscan monks, it was dedicated to "Our Lady of the Seven Joys."

Five years later, on July 31st, 1921, the little white church was blessed by Archbishop Henry Joseph O'Leary. He gave it a new name - St. Mary - and dedicated it to "Our Lady of the Mines." Beginning in 1925, Beverly was served from the Sacred Heart Parish and then, in 1930 it became part of the Cathedral Parish and St. Joseph's Seminary. From 1935 to 1940, Rev. Father Louis Charles Walravens, o. Praem, came regularly to Beverly. For about a year early in the 1940s, the Oblates of Mary Immaculate, residing at the Provincial House on 110th Street, took charge of the Beverly mission. In 1942, the Redemptorist Fathers from St. Alphonsus Parish were summoned by Archbishop John Hugh MacDonald to serve the Beverly Mission and seven years later the Franciscan monks again undertook to minister to the Beverly Catholic population.

In September 1951 the church paid $1,000 to Mrs. L. Ostapiuk for the land and building situated at 4603 118 Avenue. The transaction was completed the following month when a further $500 was paid and the building became St. Mary's Parish Hall. In July 1953, the old St. Mary's Church was sold and improvements began at the Parish Hall to make it suitable for a church.

St. Mary's was established as a parish with Rev. Henry B. Peet as its resident pastor August 15th, 1953. Rev. Peet moved into the Parish Hall, where he lived until 1961. Water and sewer systems arrived in Beverly at last and, at a cost to the congregation of $900, they were installed in the Parish buildings. With tremendous growth in Beverly's population, it was only a matter of time until the 160 seat temporary church in the Hall site was no longer sufficient. And so in 1955 the Beverly Catholic Church purchased four lots at the southwest corner of 40th Street and 115th Avenue from Henri and Yvonne Prince for $3,000. A building fund was started in June 1959 and, in just seven months, it netted more than $5,000 from parishioners and supporters.

The new church, a modern open beam brick and frame structure with seating for 500 and a rectory wing, was designed by George A. Jellinek. It was built for the modest sum of $75,000 under the guidance of Rev. Cornelius Landrigan and blessed and dedicated to St. Paul the Apostle on Sunday, December 16th, 1962 by Very Rev. Edmond F. Donahue, Dean of Edmonton Centre. Rev. Landrigan celebrated the first mass in the new St. Paul's church with Rev. Donald Steinn of St. Edmond's Parish as master of ceremonies and music provided by seminarians from St. Joseph's Seminary.

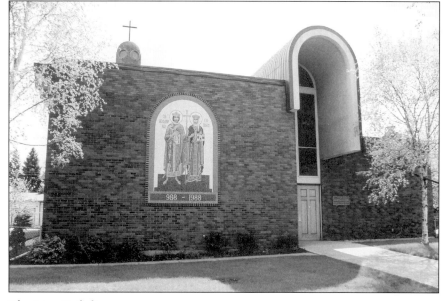

Ukrainian Catholic Protection Parish, May 2000

Ukrainian Catholic Parish of the Protection of the Blessed Virgin Mary

Ukrainian Catholics in Beverly celebrated their first Divine Liturgy in 1936 at the home of A. Holyk, a service conducted by Basilian Fathers. In 1950, Rev. Dr. M. Sopuliak was appointed to serve the Beverly Ukrainian Catholic community and mass was then celebrated every Sunday in the Roman Catholic St. Mary's Parish. The following year, the Ukrainian Catholic Parish of the Protection of the Blessed Virgin Mary was instituted and that summer Rev. Basil Martynyk was appointed parish priest.

In 1953, with Rev. Dr. Paul Hradiuk as parish priest, the congregation purchased the old St. Mary's Church at 3635 116th Avenue from the Roman Catholic parish for $4,500. Renovations and an addition with a total value of

$3,000 were completed by parish member L. Fedun. By the mid 1950s, the parish had grown to more than 70 families. That growth continued into the 1960s, putting pressure on the tiny old church. At the annual general meeting in 1962, the membership decided to erect a new and larger place of worship on the same site.

Over the next two years, the congregation managed to raise $29,630, with 40 per cent of the total contributed by the Ukrainian Catholic Women's League of the Parish. A sod turning ceremony, led by Bishop Neil Savaryn, was held August 21, 1964 and construction began two days later. Just nine months later - May 1, 1965 - the church was blessed by Bishop Savaryn during a Pontifical Divine Liturgy.

Bethlehem Lutheran Church, May 2000

Bethlehem Lutheran Church

The Bethlehem congregation was founded by Rev. H.J. Boettcher, Minister at Grace Lutheran Church. His Walther League started a Sunday School in a deserted store at 66th Street and 120th Avenue in the late 1920s and, in 1932, the first services in both English and German were conducted in the store. Two years later, property at the corner of 119th Avenue and 65th Street was purchased and the first services were conducted in a new place of worship in 1935. Formal organization of the congregation was February 20th, 1938 and later that year the Bethlehem Ladies Aid was established. The group then organized as the Lutheran Women's Missionary League (LWML) on December 21st, 1951.

By that time, the original church was proving too small and so a larger structure was built on three lots at the corner of 118th Avenue and 59th Street. The first services were held in the basement of the new church December 20th, 1953 and dedication services were May 15th, 1955. But, with a rapidly growing demand, that church, too, proved inadequate and in May 1961 a building committee was appointed. Since the property around the church was too small for expansion, the congregation decided to relocate.

Land at 47th Street and 117th Avenue was purchased in May 1962 and work on the new building commenced at the end of June 1963. The latest Bethlehem Lutheran Church was dedicated December 1st, 1963 by Rev. W.P. Schoepp. Nine years later, the congregation became self-supporting - the first time since the 1938 beginning that no subsidy was requested from the District.

In 1980, the church sponsored a school in the church using the Accelerated Christian Education (ACE) curriculum. Initial enrolment was 43 students from Kindergarten to Grade 12 taught by two teachers. The following school year, the Agape Training Centre shifted to the vacated Beverly Heights School and, until the Ministry was closed in 1988, offered Christian instruction to more than 200 students.

The congregation determined in 1993 that the existing building needed to be updated and a feasibility study found the site suitable for an expansion. A building drive was launched in 1994 and, over the next three years, it gathered more than $300,000 for the project. Using volunteer labour under the Lutheran Church-Canada's "Labourers for Christ" program, construction began in May 1996. The renovated existing building and addition were dedicated October 23rd, 1997.

Marantha Christian Reformed Church, May 2000

Marantha Christian Reformed Church

The Marantha Christian Reformed Church of Beverly was organized April 30th, 1953 and early services were conducted in the Beverly Theatre and Slovak National Hall. A church booklet commemorating the 25th anniversary of the congregation in 1978 recalled the interior of the hall left much to be desired. "A platform sufficed as 'pulpit' and some planks lying on crates supplemented the few pews we used to sit on." The consistory quickly decided to buy 125 chairs and, in just a few weeks, they were filled to capacity. Running out of room, but with precious few dollars available, the congregation came together at an August 17, 1953 meeting to evaluate a proposal from the consistory for a new structure with at least 500 seats and a future capacity of upwards of 700 with the construction of balconies. It passed unanimously.

Five lots near 119th Avenue and 47th Street were purchased and a Building Committee established. The Canadian Emergency Building Fund granted $10,000 to the project - the maximum available. Nick Spronk was invited to design a suitable structure and the budget for the entire project, including furnishings, was set at $35,000. At a congregational meeting November 9th, 1953, postcard sized sketches of the interior and exterior were circulated and, such was the enthusiasm of the gathering that plans were unanimously approved and every wage-earner donated a week's pay and many volunteered their labour.

Construction began immediately with Nick Niemansverdriet, John Fortuin and Nick Spronk as foreman. Materials were acquired from wherever possible; the pulpit, balcony, doors and baptismal font were made of solid oak taken from an old house that stood on 107th Street near 99th Avenue (the present site of the Federal Building). The wrought iron light fixtures were crafted over a kitchen stove by Andries Kamphuis, a member of the congregation who had been an old country blacksmith and welder. Kamphuis also molded the front door handles with the leaders G M Z O, the initials for the prayer under which the congregation lived: "God zy met ons." (The Lord be with us.)

On Christmas Eve, 1953 a ferocious windstorm knocked down the first beams and damaged the floor. Volunteers were on the site Christmas Day, working to repair the damage. Propelled by such remarkable devotion, the building was virtually complete the following spring. Rev. John Hanenburg dedicated the structure at 11905 47th Street on September 9th, 1954 and offered a prayer of thanksgiving. In the Dutch tradition that says a church tower is not complete without a weathercock, charter member D. Schuurman placed one there, prompting Beverlyites to call the house of worship "the church with the rooster on top."

Beverly Alliance Church

With help from Beulah Alliance Church, the first outreach programs were held in Beverly in the early 1960s. On January 24th , 1965, services conducted by Beulah's Rev. Dave Tjart, began at the Beverly Crest Motor Inn with 36 in attendance for the Sunday School. Services were moved to Beacon Heights

Beverly Alliance Church, May 2000

School May 8th , 1966 and the Vacation Bible School attracted 347 participants. In the meantime, the church's new home, at 12235 50th Street, was under construction. On the Sunday before Christmas 1966, the congregation moved into the basement of the church for its Christmas program, with parishioners sitting on folding chairs. With the building near completion, dedication ceremonies were held April 9th, 1967. A expansion began in August 1983 and was completed in September 1985.

Other Beverly places of worship over the years have included the Beulah Church of Jesus Christ at 11901 50th Street, Beverly Church of the Nazarene at 3831 116th Avenue, Gurdwara Nanaksar (Sikh temple) at 4603 118th Avenue and Foursquare Gospel Church at 11940 47th Street.

A Place to Live and Play

Elizabeth and Henny Krol, near 119th Avenue and 45th Street, 1954

Photo courtesy Dirk Krol

*F*or nearly the first half of the 20th century, life in Beverly resembled that of many prairie towns. Homeowners dug their own wells, the toilet was out back and electricity was a luxury. Light came from oil lamps, heat from coal-fired stoves. Most everyone had a vegetable garden, a few chickens, some ducks and geese and perhaps a cow and a pig or two. Going into downtown Edmonton was called "a trip into the city" and, to get there, those not fortunate enough to have an automobile trudged over to the Highlands streetcar line at 112th Avenue and 62nd Street.

From the beginning right through the 1940s, roads in Beverly were simple dirt affairs, except 118th Avenue, or Alberta Avenue as it was then known, which boasted a bed of gravel. Because of the high water table, soil conditions, the cycles of freezing and thawing and mining in the area, the roadways would continuously sink and required frequent attention to remain passable. The dips along 118th Avenue between 40th and 44th Streets were always good topics

A Beverly calf, circa 1940

Photo courtesy
Irene MacLowick

for discussion, with stories of holes so big they nearly swallowed cars, told in the grand spirit of fish tales that got bigger with every telling.

"That mud, it was up to your knees, when it rained, it was everywhere," remembers Walter MacDonald, who has called Beverly home since he was born here in 1927. "You could always count on the mud." Wooden sidewalks lined many of the streets and, with the boggy conditions, were greatly appreciated by residents and merchants. But down 118th Avenue, wooden sidewalks were few and far between and so council decided to apply cinders to help alleviate that sinking feeling. The sharp, hard edges made for initially difficult walking (particularly for young children) but after some days of use, the surface compacted and travel was much easier.

While houses in Edmonton were sometimes large and lavish, homes in Beverly were typically modest and functional. Even today, a drive through the neighbourhood reveals an abundance of simple two and three bedroom bungalows, many under 1,000 square feet. While renovations and additions have added square footage to many of these older houses, their original utilitarian character is often still easy to discern. A few of these houses, like the one at 4602 117 Avenue, were framed using timbers from the Beverly area mines.

Residents of those days vividly recall freezing cold nights in these one and two storey farm houses with no insulation and no central heating. "We'd put hot bricks at the bottom of the bed at night because it was so cold," remembers Harold Jinks, whose family lived in a small house at 3829 112 Avenue. "We could see through the ceiling of that darned house. The water in the pail used to freeze overnight, even though it was next to the stove."

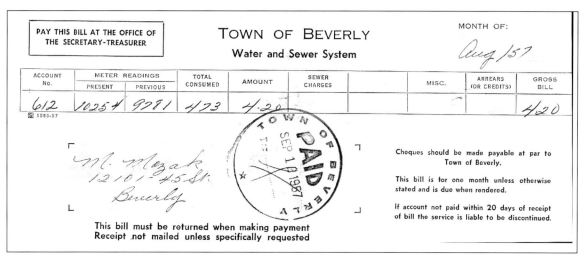

Artifact courtesy Bill Mozak

Usually there was just one or two houses on an entire block - like it was when MacDonald's family moved into the district in 1924. They purchased five lots near present day 111th Avenue and 36th Street and he recalls: "The next neighbour was a little more than a holler away." The chance to own an acreage rather than just a lot proved a lure in the 1920s and it wasn't until the boom after World War II that the big parcels were chopped into smaller pieces.

All these years later, Walter and his wife Joyce are still living on the property, now subdivided into 16 lots. But his memories of Beverly as a young boy remain vivid. "It was a great place to grow up because everybody knew each other and everybody looked out for each other."

Beverly was a family community, nurtured as a place where people knew their neighbours and felt safe allowing their children to play in the streets or in the

Artifact courtesy Bill Mozak

fields. The incidence of crime in Beverly was actually much lower than Edmonton year after year prior to amalgamation. Everybody knew everybody and, if you wanted to get away with something, you were less likely to try it in Beverly.

CODE	DO—Domestic WR—Water EA—Arrears TOT—Total Amount	CALGARY POWER LTD. 140 - 1st AVE. WEST, CALGARY CONSUMER'S STATEMENT—DOMESTIC SERVICE					
Present Meter Reading	Previous Meter Reading	Consumption	Discount	CODE	Gross Am't If Not Paid By Discount Date	Net Amount If Paid By Discount Date
27 27	21 90	5 37	60 D		13 06	12 46

CALGARY POWER AGENT
JAN 13 1951

I have no gun, yet my renown
Keeps thieves and prowlers from coming 'round.
SAVE YOUR DISCOUNT

Bill Mozak, BEVERLY, Alta.	ACCT. No. BV 3756	FROM Oct. 17, TO Dec. 16, 1950.
MONTHLY SERVICE CHGE.	BILLING PERIOD	DISCOUNT EXPIRES Jan. 13
12107-45 St.		

E. & O. E.

*Elizabeth and Henny
Krol, 1953*

Photo courtesy Dirk Krol

Community organizations contributed enormously to the fabric of the community - right from the very beginning. Beverly's first community organization was formed in the mid-1920s. The first meetings of the Beverly Citizens League were held at local churches and the second floor of the Beverly Town Hall. But the Beverly Citizens League was a casualty of the Great Depression and it wasn't until 1949 that the Beverly Community League was formed.

Beverly Women's Franchise Club held its first gathering in 1907, setting the stage for decades of dedicated community service by women in other groups such as the Busy Housewives' Club. Noteworthy community groups over the years included the 100-member Beverly Horticultural Association (with its famous annual exhibition), the Citizens' League, the Lions Club, the Tennis Club, (which operated a court near 118th Avenue and 40th Street), the Businessmen's Association, the Triple "C" Club, the Beverly Sports Committee and the Beverly Dramatic Club. "Once you live here, you don't want to leave," explains Stella Skrzekowski, who began calling Beverly home in 1958. "There is a spirit here that really is special."

Beverly Dramatic Club

City of Edmonton Archives,
EA-160-1725

BEVERLY'S NEIGHBOURHOODS

Beverly Heights

Beverly Heights took its first steps in 1913 when River Lots 36, 38 and 40 were divided into lots and put on the market. That land now comprises the area from 34th Street to 50th Street and the North Saskatchewan River to 118th Avenue. Today, Beverly Heights is 77 per cent residential and of that, 72 per cent are single unit dwellings. Most of these homes were built during the boom of

Beverly Heights, May 2000

the 1950s and their very orientation provides a fascinating physical clue that, even 40 years later, says Edmonton and Beverly were indeed separate entities. Houses in Beverly Heights are avenue-oriented and do not match those in adjoining Highlands, where the houses are oriented to the street.

Beacon Heights

Beacon Heights was incorporated in 1913, along with land to the south, as the Village of Beverly. There's some uncertainty about the source of the name Beacon Heights but it may well have been named by an enthusiastic land promoter sometime around 1910. The neighbourhood has as its boundaries 50th Street on the west, 34th Street on the east, 118th Avenue on the

Beacon Heights, May 2000

south and 122nd Avenue on the north. Today, 84 per cent of the neighbourhood is residential with 77 per cent of them single unit dwellings, mostly constructed in the 1950s. Higher density housing was constructed between 1960 and 1980 near 118th Avenue.

Rundle Heights

In 1882, the area now called Rundle Heights was just two land holdings at the northeast corner of the Edmonton settlement. In those days, the flat land near

*Rundle Heights,
May 2000*

111th Avenue was under cultivation and much of the area remained agricultural for another 80 years. Residential development in Rundle Heights began in the neighbourhood's southwest and proceeded north and east in the 1960s. Single unit housing in the most easterly portion of the neighbourhood was erected in the early 1970s. Apartment and row houses were added throughout that decade along its curvilinear and cul-de-sac street pattern, a common urban design for subdivisions built after the 1960s. More than half of the dwelling units in Rundle Heights are multi-family.

Abbottsfield

The property which is now the neighbourhood of Abbottsfield was owned in 1882 by E.F. Carey, co-founder of the merchandising firm of Norris and Carey and one of Edmonton's most prominent early citizens. Since the area was east of the Town of Beverly, it persisted as a rural area until it was annexed to the city in 1961. Even then, its proximity to the Beverly land fill site and the chemical plants on the other side of the river squelched development.

*Abbottsfield,
May 2000*

As the old dump was redeveloped to become Rundle Park in the 1960s, the area north of 118th Avenue and east of 34th Street was poised for development and was given the name Abbottsfield, after Abraham Abbott, long time custodian of Beverly schools. Where once there were just fields, row housing and apartment complexes quickly sprouted - but no single family dwellings. Abbottsfield's concentration of multi-family housing make it unique among Edmonton neighbourhoods developed before 1980.

The row housing and apartments are built around a centrally located school and recreation site, home to Abbott Elementary, St. Sophia Catholic Elementary and Abbottsfield Park. The neighbourhood's best known landmark is Abbottsfield Mall, situated at the south end of the neighbourhood and fronting 118th Avenue.

Bergman

As demand for new housing continued to escalate in the economic boom of the late 1970s, the city decided to rezone the northern part of Beacon Heights and Bergman was born. Located between 34th and 50th Streets and north of 122nd Avenue to the CNR Mainline, the neighbourhood initially contained only a few single family dwellings along 122nd and 123rd Avenues, erected in the 1950s and early 1960s. The newer portion of Bergman, north of 123rd Avenue, was plotted to contain 183 single family dwellings and eight duplexes. By the time services were installed, the boom had gone bust and many of the lots sat vacant for several years before the economy rebounded in the 1980s.

A Place of Remembrance - The Beverly Cenotaph

Beverly Cenotaph Memorial Service, 1933

City of Edmonton Archives, EA-160-1168

Southwest corner of 40th Street and 118th Avenue

The Morning Bulletin reported it was a beautiful autumn afternoon when a monument "erected by the Beverly veterans institute in the memory of their comrades fallen in the war" was unveiled at three o'clock, Sunday, October 17, 1920. The grand ceremony was attended by several dignitaries, including Lt. Gov. George Brett, Brigadier-General William Griesbach, Edmonton Mayor Joe Clarke and Beverly Mayor Fred Humberstone. The cenotaph was erected in Memorial Park on two lots owned by Thomas R. Dando, the town's postmaster, and leased to the town for a period of 99 years.

Beverly contributed 170 men to the First World War effort, with 27 paying the ultimate sacrifice. The marble and concrete monument to the fallen, erected by the Beverly Veterans' Association which had been founded April 9, 1920, was the first such structure built in the Edmonton area and one of the first in the entire province. The Benediction, pronounced by Father Ivor Daniel, and the singing of the National Anthem brought the proceedings to a close, the Bulletin reported.

Beverly Memorial Service, Nov. 1, 1948

City of Edmonton Archives, EA-160-336

Etched above the names of the lost servicemen is a sketch of a heavy artillery canon and, while the canon appears at first to be an appropriate decoration for a stone surface, it turns out that it also has a local connection. Research by Thomas Court, retired curator of collections liaison at the Provincial Museum of Alberta reveals that military gun barrels were cast in a local foundry during the First World War. The foundry may well have been part of the Ottewell Coal Mine located at the east end of the CNR Railway bridge on a site now occupied by the Celanese Canada Plant. Court says the coal was ideal for foundry casting "and its use in the manufacture of gun barrels is testament to this fact. Unfortunately, all that remains to remind us of this industry is the depiction of the armament on the Beverly War Memorial."

After the Second World War, the Town doubled the size of Memorial Park with the addition of two adjoining lots and the Cenotaph moved to a more central location in the park. On Sunday, October 5, 1958, more than 1,000 persons turned out for the re-dedication of the Beverly War Memorial. A plaque bearing the names of five Beverly residents who died in the Second World War was unveiled by Mayor John Sehn. The park continues to be the scene of a memorial service every Remembrance Day. In recent years, the Norwood Legion has been responsible for this service.

Beverly's First Postmaster

Thomas R. Dando became Postmaster of Beverly in 1911, when the fledgling community was home to barely 200 souls. The earliest post office building was a wooden framed affair, situated on the north side of 118th Avenue just east of Chaplain Street (40th). Over the years, there was also a post office on the other side of the avenue, where the Drake Hotel now stands. That building was eventually moved to the west side of 40th Street and it now comprises the front part of the McClinton Motors building at 4009 118 Avenue.

Dando Block (The Red & White Store), 1937

City of Edmonton Archives, EA-160-328

Dando served in World War I and became a charter member of the Beverly Veterans' Association, eventually donating the two lots for the cenotaph. He served one term as mayor in 1918-19 and it was during his term that council eventually decided to construct the town hall. In 1924, he built the Dando Block, which was home to his Red & White General Store, at the northeast corner of 118th Avenue and 40th Street. He was just 60 years old when he died in October 1927 of an apparent heart attack, while winding up his mother's estate in Galt, Ontario. His building survived until about 1947, when it was gutted by fire and subsequently demolished.

Beverly's One-armed Postmaster

William E. Curtis, the postmaster in Beverly for 20 years to the day, came to Canada from England in 1911 to join a relative who was in the coal mining business. He enlisted in 1916 and became a member of the 194th Battalion and three years later returned from war without his left arm. After a stint of farming near Barrhead, Alberta, Curtis returned to Beverly in 1932. He was appointed postmaster October 10th, 1936, when the job was, in his words,

A one time Beverly Post Office Building in its modern incarnation, 4009 118 Avenue, May 2000

"thrust upon him" by a postal inspector named Herbert. "I didn't know beans about post office work," Curtis said upon his retirement. He also served as a member of the Beverly School Board for 14 years and Police Magistrate, President of the Edmonton Branch of War Amputations of Canada and choirmaster of the Beverly United Church Choir.

Police and Fire Service in Beverly

The need for policing in Beverly was discussed at the very first meeting of village council in June 1913 but it wasn't until later that year that Herbert J. Swainson took up his duties. The minutes of the October 13, 1913 meeting reveal that vandalism and the "indiscriminate firings of rifles etc. in the town"

Magistrate William Curtis (left) with Chief Alphonsus McIlhargey

Photo courtesy Dale McIlhargey

prompted Chairman Robert Walker to move that "a constable be appointed for such time as may be necessary." Beverly's first Chief of Police was Homer Stewart, who was appointed by town council in 1914. He was followed by Frank Walsh, appointed chief October 31, 1916. It wasn't until the 1940s that Beverly required more than one full time constable, when it grew to a force of three, then six and then eight officers by amalgamation in 1961. Police chiefs and town constables over the years included Frank Walsh, Earl Floden, Tom Johnson, Norman West, Orest Schur, Alphonsus McIlhargey, R.B. McDowell and George Hanlan.

The jail was located at the back of the town hall and long time resident Bill Mozak remembers, "Being boys, we just had to creep up to the back of the jailhouse and peer inside to see if anyone was locked up. There was also a big corral back there for stray horses and cows that the constables had rounded up."

In a working class town without a lavish policing budget, the Chiefs of Police usually used their own vehicles. For Chief McIlhargey, who served from 1951 to 1958, his patrol car was originally a green 1950 Chevrolet and later a blue 1954 Pontiac, both fitted with sirens.

Chief McIlharghey in front of jail cells, circa 1953

Photo courtesy Dale McIlhargey

Police duties at the time included more than keeping the peace. There was traffic to patrol (maximum speed limit was 25 miles per hour) and loose dogs to catch and return to their owner before the dog catcher got them. Sometimes the dogs weren't so lucky. In a 1954 report to town council, the chief reported he had shot ten stray dogs the previous week after effort to find the owners were unsuccessful. Because of the shortage of phones in the 1950s, the police station often served duty as a message centre, taking and relaying emergency messages to those citizens without a phone.

Beverly Fire Hall, circa 1968

City of Edmonton Archives, EA-20-5108

The Beverly Fire Department began life as a humble affair and it stayed that way for nearly 50 years. A story in the May 13, 1916 Edmonton Bulletin reported Beverly's purchase of a chemical fire engine from R.H. Beckle of Woodstock, Ontario. The fire engine had been bought with the condition that it perform satisfactorily and a company representative headed west for the big test. In front of a large number of spectators (on May 10, 1916), "a large bonfire was built up and lighted several times and successfully extinguished by the engine," the paper reported. "The

engine was deemed satisfactory." The new engine was used by the town's fire department, which remained a volunteer affair usually operating with just one pumper unit, right until amalgamation at the end of 1961.

Adventure on the Railway Bridge

In the days before the Beverly Bridge was opened in 1953, the only way across the river was to walk the high deck of the railway bridge. "There were about eight wooden water barrels across the bridge - four on each side," remembers long time resident Henry Walters, who was born in Beverly January 13, 1913. "If a train came when you were on the bridge you would climb into the barrel until the train passed. Dad told us one night when he came home from the mine the wind was so strong that he and the other miners had to crawl on their hands and knees across the bridge."

Clover Bar Railway Bridge

Photo courtesy Prins Family

Hockey in Beverly

It's not there anymore, but for a group of young men in 1934, the Beverly Skating Rink at the northwest corner of 118th Avenue and 40th Street was truly a rink of dreams. Built by several men including Glenn Wilson, the rink utilized the run off from the Beverly mine, pumped by a donkey engine to flood the ice. The ice was the primary playing surface for the Bush Mine Tigers, the team that won the Coughlin Cup (the Commercial League Championship) on March 15, 1934, beating Hillas Electric Black Hawks 2-1 in the third and deciding game.

One of the last surviving members of that winning team is Harold Jinks, who scored the winning goal with just eight seconds to play. Jinks was born in 1913 and moved to Beverly in 1915. He recalls the Beverly rink was made out of a slough. "We used to pump water out of the Beverly mine ditch which ran right along 40th and flood it. Then we'd put our boards up and play some hockey.

Bush Mine Hockey Team 1933/34 (Back row from left) Frank Glossop (Secretary), Harold Jinks, Paul Guenette, Bill Danilowich, Fred Philip, Ken Campbell (Manager), (Front row from left) George Campbell, Ted Mottershed, Herbert Hanson.

City of Edmonton Archives, EA-160-1589

Newspaper article, 1934

Article courtesy Harold Jinks

We were just a bunch of hillbillies having fun," he laughs.

The Beverly Athletic Club team began play in the regional commercial league in 1931/32 and, in 1934, the team was sponsored by the Bush Mine and became the Bush Mine Tigers. The Tigers played until the 1937/38 season.

Sports Champions

For a small community, Beverly generated more than its share of championship teams. Building on the achievement of the Bush Mine Tigers, several other sports teams won big, including the Beverly Athletics and then the Beverly Drakes (sponsored by the Drake Hotel), a men's intermediate team that captured the Alberta Baseball Championships three consecutive times in the early 1950s. Another Beverly team called the Edmonton Rotary Midgets won the Northern Alberta Midget Baseball Championship in 1959 and a year later a team sponsored by Beverly Welding won the Edmonton Men's Fastball Championship.

BEVERLY PAYS HONOR TO ITS HOCKEY TEAM

Champion Bush Mine Tigers Guests at Banquet, Dance

Beverly citizens turned out en masse Thursday night to the banquet in the United church which was held in honor of Mr. K. S. Campbell and his Bush Mine Tigers, winners of the Coughlin cup, emblem of the Commercial league hockey championship. Mayor Gerry, accompanied by Mrs. Gerry, presided and proposed the toast to the Bush Mine Tigers. This was responded to by Mr. Cecil Hightower, president of the hockey club. Manager K. S. Campbell, Secretary F. Glossop, Captain Harold Jinks and Vice-captain Paul Guenette also spoke expressing their appreciation of the support they had received during the season and of the fine public recognition of their suc[...] in the banquet and enterta[...] Mr. H. Haverstock pro[...] st "To the Ladies" an[...] ion made a very [...] on their behalf [...] vited were

As hundreds of families poured into the district in the 1950s, the minor hockey program expanded dramatically many boys and girls participated in the sports programming that became one of the most utilized in the entire Edmonton area. Among the many successful teams over the years was the Beverly Heights Peewee hockey team, which won the 1977 Taber Invitational Peewee Hockey Tournament. That year, the team also travelled to California to compete in the West Covina International Christmas Peewee Hockey Tournament and then repeated as champions at Taber in 1978. Several Beverly players made it to the National Hockey League including Harold Schnepts and brothers Gary and Kenny Yaremchuk.

COMMUNITY LEAGUES

Beverly and Beverly Heights

Out of a desire to develop a playground and organize fund raisers for the Beverly boys softball team, the first meeting of the Beverly Community League was held in 1949 at the Beverly United Church. R.A. Wright was elected president. But it proved difficult to persuade townsfolk to participate. In desperation, the 1953 executive postponed all programs indefinitely, hoping their action would awaken in the community a sense of urgency. It didn't work.

Beverly Heights Community League, May 2000

Five years later, the Beverly Home and School Association revitalized the community league and a 1958 communique in the Beverly Page proclaimed in bold type: "WANTED - 1000 FAMILIES." Residents were urged to "Invest One Five-spot for 12 Months of Entertainment." The campaign was successful and the following year the Beverly Community League and the

Lions and Optimists Clubs joined to build a rink and rink house at Floden Park.

Buoyed by the response, a campaign was launched to raise funds for a recreation complex. With a boost from a recreation grant from the provincial government, construction on the Beverly Recreation Centre at 40th Street south of 111th Avenue commenced in 1961. The centre officially opened in November 1962 - just ten months after Beverly amalgamated with Edmonton. When that happened, the facility passed into the city's ownership. It wasn't until September 1978 that the building was purchased back from the city by the Beverly Heights Community League. The price tag was $195,000. In 1960, the Beverly Community League became the Beverly Community Recreation League and in 1965 it was renamed the Beverly Heights Community League. By the end of the 1960s, it was the largest community league by membership in the city. With the high demand for facilities, the community league proposed to build an addition to its hall but opposition from nearby residents scuttled the plan and so the recreation centre was purchased instead.

Tom and Millie Cross

In the late 1960s and 1970s, Tom and Millie Cross were known as "the couple that owns the rink." Ice makers, caretakers, sports organizers, concessionaires and Jacks-of-all-trades, the couple exemplified the spirit of giving that built the Beverly Heights Community League from just a few memberships to the largest in Edmonton and grew the minor sports program from a handful of teams to more than 20 between 1960 and 1980. The rink shack they used became known as "Uncle Tom's Cabin."

Tom and Millie Cross

Photo courtesy
Millie Cross

With his excavation business operational only in the warmer months, Cross was able to devote thousands of hours every year to the community. In a 1978 Edmonton Journal article, he explained that his own experience as a boy

107

taught him the value of participation. "I didn't have the advantage of organized hockey as a boy, and I would argue you can't over-organize at the minor levels to develop talent."

Tom explained that the couple's children Jim, John and Sharon had also benefited enormously from participation in community league activities. A tournament that Tom started for Mite hockey in the 1970s was later named the Tom Cross Tournament. Tragically, Tom died in a car crash in 1997 while returning from the American sun belt.

The Beverly Heights Variety Show

Gabe Keller and Peter Chmiliar perform, 1977

Photos courtesy Beverly Heights Community League

At 30 years and counting, the Beverly Heights Community League Variety Show is Edmonton's longest running and one of its most successful community fund raisers. Powered entirely by volunteer effort, the variety show turns the community league hall into a great big laugh festival for a few delightful evenings every February and March. The event, which began in 1971, has garnered a reputation for suggestive risque humour and usually sells out every performance.

The idea for the show germinated in the fertile mind of Judy Jacobs who, with her husband Lawrence, went to see a similar variety show in the Edmonton community of Wellington Park. That night, Judy just said, "Why don't we do that in Beverly?" And so they did and the first year's four performances sold out all 1,200 seats at $4.50 a ticket. It was the start of an Edmonton legend.

In its 30 years of operation, the show has generated hundreds of thousands of dollars for the community; revenue that has allowed the community league to purchase its building from the city, expand the facility and sponsor all manner of sports teams and community activities. "We couldn't have done what we have done without the variety show," notes Cornel Rusnak, Beverly Heights Community League President. "But beyond that, it brings people in the community together and gives them a sense of belonging, it helps neighbours become friends, it gives Beverly a long term source of income. And it is one hell of a lot of fun."

Over the years, its skits have sometimes stepped over the edge of good taste, prompting a few protests, some critical media coverage and declining attendance in the late 1980s. But as the show has begun to reach a new generation, all that has turned around and in 2000 the dozen performances were completely sold out. "It's been great to see," Lawrence Jacobs says. "It's great to see people blossom as performers - and let's not forget that many of them have never performed professionally."

Don Cook and Peter Chmiliar perform, 1980 (left)

Ari Hocksema and Dr. Sigmund Fraud perform, 1995 (top)

Will Moellering and Ken Pawluk perform, 2000 (bottom)

While other community leagues more recently have been forced to rely on bingos and casinos to pay the bills, Beverly Heights has a fund raiser that draws volunteers, not repels them. The list of those who have given their time over the years reaches into the hundreds and many of them have been helping out for 20 years and more. They include members of the Beverly Active Seniors Society, who prepare a Ukranian style dinner for show patrons on some nights. "Now, when I tell people that I'm with the Beverly Heights Community League they often say, 'Oh yes, the Beverly Heights Variety Show.' No matter where I go, I run into people who have been to the show at one time or other over the 30 years," Rusnak says. "The variety show is a real point of pride for this community."

Beacon Heights and Abbottsfield Community Leagues

The Beverly Community League split into the Beverly Heights and Beacon Heights Community

Leagues in 1965. The first president of Beacon Heights was Sam Parker. Beverly Heights retained the community grounds on 111th Avenue while Beacon Heights operated a rink and clubhouse at Jubilee Park and went shopping for a community hall. With the assistance of the Busy Housewives Society, a fund raising drive netted more than $6,500 in just one year. The new hall, the Avalon Theatre building at 4418 118th Avenue, was opened in 1971.

A new $104,000 Jubilee Park clubhouse with dressing rooms, a meeting room and kitchen was finished in 1975. That year, residents of Abbottsfield, a new development east of Beacon Heights, formed their own community league. Two years later, Abbottsfield was left out in the cold when the City of Edmonton decided to concentrate its resources on facilities in Rundle Heights Park. The need for rejuvenation of programs at Beacon Heights led to the amalgamation of the leagues under the name Beacon Heights. Under the revised objectives of the hybrid league, emphasis was placed on family activities but there were to be recreational, cultural, social and leisure programs for all age groups.

Beacon Heights Hall, May 2000

Jubilee Park

North of 120th Avenue between 42nd and 43rd Streets

When the provincial government announced grants to municipalities to celebrate Alberta's 50th anniversary in 1955, Beverly at long last had the dollars to turn the old Beverly Mine site into a park. Using the dollars from the Jubilee grant program, Beverly purchased the land that had been occupied by the Beverly Limited Mine and Beverly Jubilee Park was born. John Sehn, who was mayor at the time, recalls that to develop a park, the town had to demolish the mine tipple and relied heavily on volunteer labour to get the job done. The

outdoor skating rink was built, playground equipment was installed and trees were planted, all by volunteers.

Three years later the town opened the Beverly Jubilee Park Community Rink. Speaking to a crowd gathered for the opening ceremonies February 2nd, 1958, Mayor Sehn said the rink with accommodation for ice skating and hockey "filled a long felt need in the area." The Town had built the rink, outside fence and rink house, installed flood lights, heating equipment, washroom facilities and a concession, both all for $7,200 - a price thought by some to be impossible. Roger Bourassa was named the first rink attendant. The word Beverly was dropped from the park's name in 1989 because the community league was concerned the original name was too easily confused with the Beverly Heights community.

Mucha Rink

When Bill Mucha began flooding part of his spacious backyard for a skating rink, he started a Beverly tradition that stretched over more than 20 years. Bill and his wife Tillie arrived in Beverly in the early 1940s from the Thorsby area, buying a huge parcel of land just off 48th Street and 116th Avenue. Bill, who was a carpenter by trade, had owned and operated a sawmill and a grain mill business as well as several farms. He helped build several Beverly houses and

Skating at the Mucha Rink, circa 1955

Photos courtesy Mucha family

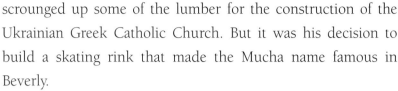

The Broomball Team at Mucha Rink (Beverly Heights School in the background)

Photo courtesy Sofie Rybie

scrounged up some of the lumber for the construction of the Ukrainian Greek Catholic Church. But it was his decision to build a skating rink that made the Mucha name famous in Beverly.

His rink featured a cozy heated shack and amplifiers for night music. There was a ten cent charge, although mothers with pre-school children were let in for free during the afternoons. Evenings were fun nights with hockey games and public skating and on Sundays adults played broomball, while hundreds more came to watch the teams compete. Two women's teams captained by Sophie Rybie and Jennie Bodnar were particular fan favourites.

Hubert Hollingworth

Hubert Hollingworth took the photograph on the cover of this book, an image capturing a row of coal trucks lined up in front of the Beverly Coal Company. If you look closely, you'll see the drivers, standing on the running boards; working men doing a working class job. Capturing the "working class heroes" was a favourite pursuit for Hollingworth. From 1924 until his retirement in 1976, he chronicled the life of Edmonton with an eye for a captivating image guided by his heart.

Then, his work not yet complete, he began working at the City of Edmonton Archives - copying images, many of them from his lifetime behind the lens. As well, he gave slide shows to groups like the Society for the Retired and Semi-Retired, regaling gatherings with anecdotes about camera gear that didn't work, recalcitrant subjects and the whims of weather and light. Hollingworth was among the first in the world to take aerial pictures but he is best remembered for his images of common people that captured the very essence of life. Sorting through the grand collection at the City of Edmonton Archives, Hollingworth's love for the common man shines through. By all accounts, the craft came to him naturally. His grandfather had operated a photo studio in England in the late 1800s.

Hubert Hollingworth

Hubert was born in 1912 in Lloydminster, Alberta. At just age 12, he came to Edmonton to apprentice with Bell Studios. While still in his teens, he took to the air with bush pilot friend Wilfrid "Wop" May, leaning out the open cockpit of a Tiger Moth biplane, clicking away, the wind tearing through his fine blond hair. During the lean days of the Great Depression, Hollingworth survived by ranching at his father Harry's Royal Silver Fox Ranch, raising fox, chinchillas and pigeons on about a block of land around their house at 12214 42nd Street. There was a sign on the property that read "No Dogs Allowed." The barking would alarm the female foxes, prompting them to sometimes eat their young.

Hubert Hollingworth married Violet Faulkner in 1936 and the couple moved into the back of his studio at 118th Avenue and 95th Street. They had one daughter - Lucille Molyneux, who resides in British Columbia's Lower Mainland. The lean years during the Second World War only inspired Hubert's creativity and, when he couldn't obtain colour film stock, Violet hand-coloured their home movies. With the war still underway, Hubert closed the shop and took a job as aerial photographer for the U.S. Army engineers building the Alaska Highway. He later worked for Edmonton's famous McDermid Studios and took aerial and society photos for the Edmonton Journal and Edmonton Bulletin. Beginning in 1954 he worked for the Edmonton office of the federal government's Department of Supply and Services but he kept clicking the shutter, capturing an Edmonton that most other photographers declined to deem important.

*Ice harvesting on the
North Saskatchewan
River, circa 1938*

City of Edmonton Archives,
EA-160-319

*Royal Silver Fox
Ranch, 1931*

City of Edmonton
Archives, EA-160-695

"The Hollingworth collection gives us images of Edmonton that we just wouldn't have otherwise," says city archivist Bruce Ibsen. "We have people coming in here all the time that find the image they need - taken by Hubert Hollingworth. It's a great tribute to the man and to his legacy." A short biography accompanying a binder of his images at the city archives offers that "a reflection of his unpretentious nature and style is captured in his photographs. We can view a rural, more relaxed Edmonton in his work; an Edmonton that would occasionally be jolted out of its somnolence by events of an internal nature - like a fire, or by external realities like May Day parades and demonstrations."

His images show a photojournalist's eye for the news story, framed with the creativity of a great artist. By all accounts, he was humble about his gift and generous with his expertise. Violet passed away in 1987 and Hubert died of a heart attack a year later. He was 75 years old.

From 1976 until shortly before his death, Hollingworth copied more than 12,700 photographic images and slides for the archives and volunteer groups. The City Archives collection numbers more than 2,000 photos and ranks as the first donation of its size from a professional photographer. Many of his images captured everyday life in Beverly - and many of them illustrate this volume. The man is gone but his legacy is reaching new eyes - the greatest tribute a photographer could ask.

Lovers' Lane & Other Diversions

It doesn't take long talking with old timers to realize that, while Beverly may not have had many of the amenities of the city, people found other ways to amuse themselves. Joe Holoiday, a long time resident, remembers: "Close to Floden Park there was a lovers lane surrounded by large trees. There was a dirt trail where the lovers drove in at night. We would watch for a car to drive in, sneak under the car and plug a potato in the tail pipe, rendering the motor unstartable. Then we would shake the car and run to the river bank."

Swimming and fishing in the North Saskatchewan was a popular pastime, particularly with young boys, who often pulled goldeye, Northern Pike ("Jacks") and occasionally an enormous Sturgeon from its waters. Bill Mozak, who grew up in Beverly, remembers sneaking down to the river "to watch the girls" swimming in the nude. And I used to ride my bike everywhere, even though the roads weren't

Sturgeon taken from North Saskatchewan River, circa 1940

City of Edmonton Archives, EA-160-329

very good for bicycling." Nestor Waluk, another long time resident, recalls: "There were lots of wide open spaces and kids could roam around and explore. Pine Creek was a favourite place. We used to collect magpie and crows' eggs and sell them for five cents each to the government."

Beverly's Boogie-Woogie Bugle Boys

Over the years Beverly has been home to many accomplished musicians. One of the most famous is Richard Chernesky, a guitarist who toured western Canada many times and in the '60's played with Gaby Haas and the Bam Dance Gang on CFRN TV. Chernesky also played with Ian Tyson on the television show Sun Country. He was honoured in 1997 by the Alberta Country and Western Association for 40 years of making music.

Don Yuzwenko (also known as Dr. Boogie) on piano and John Hunter on drums have been playing together for almost thirty years. They are accomplished musicians who have worked with many famous artists and are known to be forerunners in boogie-woogie and blues music. They are still active in the music business and continue to play and tour.

Marvin Yakoweshen is another musician originally from Beverly. He is recognized to be one of the finest saxophone players in Edmonton and continues to play and tour with several groups. From a tiny community "Built on Coal," countless musicians have been nurtured and have fashioned a life built on melody.

Merchants & Businesses

Pausing at Hunter Store, circa 1925

Photo courtesy Hunter Family

Since the beginning, 118th Avenue has been the business location of choice in Beverly. Originally known as Alberta Avenue, the thoroughfare was at first little more than cart tracks through the boggy terrain. Grading and fill in 1916 brought the road some much needed stability and, with the addition of wooden sidewalks, people began to stop and shop at the grocers and other early merchants. In those formative years, citizens usually walked or rode their horses to purchase provisions at the local merchants - either on 118th Avenue, 114th Avenue or 50th Street. These owner-operated businesses were mostly diminutive affairs, intimately connected with the residents. Everybody was on a first name basis and goods were often bought "on account."

Unfortunately, the face of 118th Avenue has changed dramatically and hardly any physical remnants of those early business ventures survive. Now all that remains are the stories and a few precious photographs, mostly from family collections.

Danilowich Store, circa 1912

Photo courtesy
Ann Shobbrook

THE GROCERS

Danilowich Store
4508 118 Avenue

Dan and Anastasia Danilowich and their families arrived in Beverly in 1912. Dan had been born in Toorod, Ukraine on December 24, 1883 and, while still a teenager, was drafted into the Austrian Army, where he rose to the rank of lieutenant in three years' service. He married 19-year-old Anastasia Proch February 23, 1908 and the couple and their families left for Canada in June of that year. They settled in Manley, Alberta and, in 1910 through 1912, Dan and his brother-in-law worked with a team of oxen laying track from Edson through Entwistle, Carrot Creek and Carvel.

In 1912 Dan moved his family to Beverly where he worked as pit boss in the Humberstone mine. But, in the fledgling community, Danilowich apparently realized the potential of the retail business and he and his brother John constructed the first general store in Beverly. The store boasted an ice house at the back, where huge blocks of ice were stored to keep meat and perishables fresh. The family lived above the store, which opened at eight in the morning and closed at 10 in the evening. In these cramped living quarters they raised 13 children, born between 1909 and 1933. They lost four of their children while still infants and son Michael died when he was just five.

The first post office in Beverly was started in the warehouse attached to the store but later was moved to a building at 40th Street and 118th Avenue. Long time residents remember the Danilowich dog, Teddy, would often fetch the mail at the new post office. "Mr. Dan", as he was known to locals, spoke several languages fluently, including German, Ukrainian, Polish, Russian, Hungarian and English and he was frequently used as a translator. His hobby was carpentry and he particularly loved to build houses and he also helped construct the Night & Day Cafe, Transit Hotel and Northwest Industries.

Behind the store was a garden and a few animals - a cow, chickens and geese. Anastasia often baked buns, donuts and often called the children in on a cold winter day for hot soup or anything that she had to warm them up when they were on their way home from school. In 1930, the depression caused extreme hardship in the community and unpaid bills forced the closure of the store. Eight years later, Kelly Douglas and H.H. Cooper Wholesale grocers offered backing to reopen the business. Danilowich then operated the store until 1952, three years after Anastasia died on October 29, 1949. He retired to his beloved carpentry and rest in the garden and lived to be 85 years old. He died July 29, 1969.

Beverly General Store
3904 118 Avenue

This store, operated by the Hunter family, was typical of a general store in Beverly in the 1920s and 30s. The Hunters lived right next door and their business was one of the few Beverly retailers to survive the depression. Many Beverly families owed the Hunters a debt of gratitude for their support during the hard times.

Beverly General Store, circa 1925

Photo courtesy
Hunter Family

Adeline and John Hunter with their family Margaret, Rendall, and Alex moved from Strathcona to Beverly in 1919, when the Hunters purchased the Beverly General Store and the living quarters above. The structure was situated at the southeast corner of 118th Avenue and 39th Street. But fire broke out in 1921 and, to get back in operation quickly, John decided to construct adjacent to a warehouse he owned on the north side of 118th. The story goes that within days the store

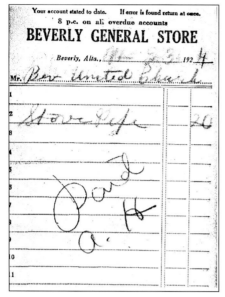

Beverly General Store receipt, 1924

Photo courtesy Beverly United Church

Oleksys Store, 114th Avenue & 47th Street, 1929

Photo courtesy Adelaide and Mary Hnidan

was open again and the family soon moved into a house built right next to the store.

Hunter's store was great gathering place for young and old. In the winter the activity was sitting around the pot bellied coal heater playing cards and swapping stories. In the summer the boys enjoyed marbles and games outside. Early on school mornings, older boys often stopped at the store to ask for Mr. Hunter's help with their math homework.

Rendall and Alex attended the Beverly Central School while Margaret went to the University of Alberta and became a school teacher. She taught in Beverly for two years. In 1937, John Hunter gave up the grocery business for farming. He sold the store and moved to a farm near Alberta Beach and died in 1942. The structure remained a general store under four more owners before the building was demolished in 1965.

When Canada went to war Rendall joined the Royal Canadian Air Force and was stationed in Newfoundland. Alex joined the Canadian Army and was wounded in action in April 1945 while in Holland. He remained in hospital two weeks and was back on the front lines along the Rhine River when the war ended. Upon their return to Canada, Rendall and Alex both bought land and settled in Beverly and their mother came to live with them . Rendall worked in the office of the Beverly Coal Mine. Alex worked in the oil fields until he started his own business, Hunters Delivery, which Rendall later joined.

There was also an earlier version of the Beverly General Store, operated by Alfred H. Jordan as early as 1914. Jordan's store was situated on the west side of 48th Street near 122nd Avenue.

Over the years, Beverly boasted many local grocery outlets. They included Haverstock Store located on 112th Avenue near 39th Street, Harry Waluk's Grocery at the corner of 44th Street and 118th Avenue and Nick Kliciak's Grocery at the northwest corner of 39th Street and 118th Avenue. Alex Lastiwka operated his store at 4414 118th Avenue, Walt's Grocery was on 118th Avenue near 49th Street, Oleksys Grocery was located at 114th Avenue and 47th Street and Walter's Grocery was run by Walter and Ann Tkachuk at the corner of 40th Street and 118th Avenue.

The Bus in Beverly

The Town of Beverly could not afford public transportation. It was left to residents of Beverly to walk to the end of Edmonton street car trolley line at 61st Street and 112th Avenue or to support a local private service. The first private organized bus service was offered in 1936, during the depths of the Great Depression. The Universal Bus Company commenced operations with a panel car and then grew to three buses. The company shuttled citizens from town into Edmonton until June 1947, when former Greyhound employee Kenneth Charles Durnford started his Beverly Bus Lines based out of an office at 11405 38th Street. The first bus was a 32-passenger General Motors coach and soon the service offered 20 trips on weekdays, 25 on Saturdays and 14 on Sundays.

Good for
One Adult Fare
Beverly and Union
Bus Depot
Edmonton
Beverly Bus Lines Ltd

Artifact courtesy
Gordon Wilson

Durnford died suddenly in 1951 and his wife, Ann Durnford took over and operated the company herself. She later married one of the drivers, Lester Johnson. By the late 1950s, the company boasted nine buses, which would arrive, usually at one hour intervals, at various stops throughout Beverly and proceed on to the Union Bus Depot in Edmonton. Tickets were four for 25 cents. When Beverly amalgamated with Edmonton in December 1961, Edmonton Transit began to regularly service Beverly, bringing the town's private transportation system to an end. The city offered Mrs. Johnson just $15,000 for her five Brill buses and she spent many years negotiating for a fair price.

MARKET GARDENS

When immigrants arrived in Beverly from places such as Holland and Ukraine, they brought with them an expertise in growing. It's no wonder so many started market garden farms in and around Beverly, some of which still exist today. These bounty of the land entrepreneurs included Mary Gordulic, the Vissers (Riverbend Gardens) and the Zaychuks.

Zaychuk Farms

Started as the first commercial small fruit operation in Western Canada during the Depression years, Zaychuk Farms has grown to be one of the biggest and longest operating family-run produce growers in the province. The venture was started by Stephen Michael Zaychuk, who was born in Bruzuchowicze, Poland on February 2, 1908 and emigrated to Canada in 1927. Eight years

later he married the former Mary Kobewka of Beverly and that very year he began growing strawberries on property along 44th Street. The story goes that Justice H.H. Parlee gave him $200 to start the venture and said that if the business prospered, he could repay the money, but if it did not, Zaychuk owed him nothing. In 1943, Zaychuk successfully grew Concord grapes outside and later he expanded the fruit operation by propagating fruit trees for the local climatic conditions.

Stephen & Mary Zaychuk

Photo courtesy David & Ann Zaychuk

In 1952, Zaychuk was elected to Beverly town council and then returned to office three more times, serving nine years until amalgamation with Edmonton at the end of 1961. That year, he and his son David joined as partners to form Zaychuk Nursery and Vegetable Farms Limited and acquired land east of Namao. With the guidance of Mr. Zaychuk as president, the company became the largest fresh vegetable growers in Alberta and continued to grow and prosper until a tragic end to the story. Stephen Zaychuk was killed in a car accident in Little Fort, BC on April 4, 1973. The family has carried on the tradition he so tenaciously began.

Reg Carter's Garage
4402 118th Avenue

Cars were becoming a part of everyone's life when Reginald Alfred Carter decided that his talent as a mechanic could be profitable. But what to use for a garage on 118th Avenue? No problem, he decided, and proceeded to move a garage he had built in his mother's yard at 4015 112th Avenue. He hauled the structure to the northwest corner of 44th Street and 118th Avenue. That's how Beverly Service was born.

Photo of Reg Carter's garage, circa 1945

Photo courtesy
Carter Family

Reg offered auto repairs and welding service and business was so good that he needed two tow trucks. Reg and his wife Doris Francis Burk built a small home for themselves behind the garage and raised six children. The business was sold in 1955 and the Carters retired, remaining to live in Beverly.

Prins Electric & Hardware
4408 118 Avenue

Peter Prins, the youngest of eight children of pioneer Beverly settlers Jacob and Aafje Prins, served in the Royal Canadian Air Force during the Second World War and, when he was discharged, trained as an electrician in the Veterans' Technical Training School. In 1945, Peter and Clem Sagert bought a lot with a 25 foot frontage along 118th Avenue and 44th Street from Reg Carter for $250. A small building measuring 20 feet by 20 feet was constructed as a workshop and Prins & Sagert Electric was born.

Prins bought out Sagert in 1947 and changed the business name to Prins Electric. Some three years later, the business expanded to become Prins

*Prins Electric &
Hardware*

Photo courtesy Peter Prins

Electric & Hardware Company Limited - electrical contractors and general hardware merchandisers. The store also became the collection agency for Calgary Power and the Alberta Government Telephones bills, which helped bring in customers. At this time the workshop was expanded to include living quarters - a bedroom, bathroom, kitchen and a living room - served by a well in the basement.

As electrical contractor, Peter Prins helped bring electricity to many of the older homes when Calgary Power extended their lines throughout Beverly. He also wired many of the new homes and businesses within the district. Peter's

*Prins Electric &
Hardware, 1950*

Photo courtesy Peter Prins

wife Sadie and her father, Ted Reitsma, operated the hardware store, which really was much more than that. Besides the usual assortment of hardware goods, the store also sold housewares, from china to large and small appliances, lamps, televisions and decorations.

Soon another extension was built onto the original shop, adding a section in front for the retail store area and new living quarters above. Sadie's parents, Ted and Ida, lived upstairs until 1963. The business was sold in 1972 and the property transferred in 1975. Dr. Peter Bartkus built his dentist office on the site and the practice continues to operate there.

Avalon Theatre
4418 118 Avenue

One local place of gathering was the Avalon Theatre. In 1950, Nick Ruptash and his son-in-law Don Kubalik thought about building a hotel, but looking at the economic indicators, new citizens pouring in by the car load and the forecasts for a population boom, they decided to build a 485-seat theatre and they called it the Avalon. Construction began on a large lot on the northeast corner of 45 Street and 118 Avenue in April 1950 and the building was complete in November that year.

Its neon sign was the first in Beverly and, as the only film house in the east end, the Avalon was an

Avalon Theatre, 1950s

Photo courtesy
Kubalik and Raptash
Families

immediate hit. But the market was small in Beverly and movies changed every three days. The entire family got involved with the operation of the theatre; Nick and Vera Ruptash's daughters Elsie, Mickey, Christine helped out with the ticket and popcorn sales and the cleaning and Don's brother Andy ran the projection room. It was Elsie (Don's wife) who named the theatre and she and Don lived in the apartment above it and that's where two of their children were born. Ticket prices were 15 cents for children, 25 cents for students and 45 cents for adults. A crying room for parents with young children had five seats.

With the arrival of television, business took a major hit and the theatre closed in 1958. The building then became home to several other ventures over the next several years including a bowling alley, a furniture store and a seniors' drop-in centre. Today, the remodeled building is home to the Beacon Heights Community League and is adorned by one of Beverly's famous murals - a rendering by Eastglen High School art students depicting how the street looked in the 1950s.

Drake Hotel

3945 118 Avenue

When the Drake Hotel officially opened May 26, 1950, it was touted as proof that "as far as Beverly is concerned, the boom is on." The two-storey frame and

stucco building featured 20 rooms built on an "L" shaped floor plan to give all rooms outward facing windows, a lobby, coffee shop and separate beverage rooms for men and women. Rough cedar planks covered the

Drake Hotel, May 1959

Provincial Archives of Alberta, PA-2545/2

bottom of the north and west exterior walls, with canopies over all entrances and the famous vertical H-O-T-E-L sign prominent on the second level near the 40th Street corner.

Named for the male Mallard ducks that frequented a large slough nearby, the site of the hotel was one of the most popular in the town right from the beginning. Recollections of early settlers say a livery stable was on the property at the time of the early mines. Later, the post office and then a half finished retail development stood on this spot.

The Drake Hotel was developed by a group of Edmonton businessmen and, as a May 25, 1950 Edmonton Journal article proclaimed, it was the quality of accommodation and appealing decor that made it so attractive. "Real feature of the Drake rooms is the high quality mattresses and springs. Sleeping comfort is assured every guest. All rooms are fitted with running water and all afford clothes closet space."

The hotel again made the news two years later when $10,000 was allegedly taken by two masked and armed robbers in a heist at 2 am the morning of September 21st, 1953. Night clerk Metro Westrouk was bound and gagged and the two blew the safe with explosives. The bandits fled into the night with $3,000 to $4,000 cash and cheques for $6,800. Beverly Police Chief A. McIlhargey described the safe cracking as the work of experts and said it was obviously a well-planned job as the thieves knew where to find the key to the office after binding the clerk.

In 1964, a bar with separate "Men's" and "Ladies' and Escorts" sections was added to the rear of the existing hotel. Over the years, the hotel has changed hands five times. The family of the current owner, Earl Bolichowski, purchased the hotel on May 21, 1972, investing the insurance money received when the old Donald Hotel in Grande Prairie burned to the ground.

Beverly Pharmacy
southwest corner 44 Street and 118 Avenue

Beverly Pharmacy, September 1951

Photo courtesy
Bill Lesick

William (Bill) and Winifred Lesick's Beverly Pharmacy opened August 1, 1951

and, for the next 31 years, it was a local institution. Lesick bought the business from a young Fort Saskatchewan pharmacist who had opened the store two months earlier but decided it wasn't for him. The one-storey retail block had been built as a restaurant sometime in the 1940s. For Lesick, just back from the war and fresh out of university, the pharmacy provided his first

127

opportunity to own a business. But the local economy wasn't good and the business struggled in its early days.

Yet Bill and Winnie persevered and eventually prospered. They sold the business in February 1983, a few months after Lesick had captured the federal Conservative nomination for Edmonton West. Lesick was elected as Member of Parliament in the 1984 general election. For Beverly citizens, the pharmacy became a centre of the community - and the place mothers bought their children dreaded cod liver oil and other medicines for nasty colds and gripe.

Beverly Bakery, circa 1958

Photo courtesy
Anton Jansen

Beverly Bakery
4118 and 4435 118 Avenue

Beverly Bakery began operations at 4118 118 Avenue in November 1953, the brainchild of three Dutch-Canadian bakers - Anton Jansen, Richard (Dick) Plaizier and Bob Veenstra. All three had worked extensively in the baking industry in Holland, with Plaizier boasting 25 years of baking experience. With limited capital, but an abundance of know-how, the three men rolled up their sleeves and went to work. The first day's baking went unsold, but as word spread, business grew. Beverly's side roads were so poor that a horse-drawn wagon was the only way to get through the mud on many days and so the company used one wagon and two trucks for delivery.

Artifact courtesy
Anton Jansen

By 1958, the fleet had grown to seven trucks, the horse had been retired and demand necessitated a new plant. The new $50,000 location at 4435 118th Avenue opened in March 1958, featuring as its showpiece a giant fully automatic Hubbard oven, capable of baking 500 loaves of bread per hour and turning out evenly baked cookies and pastries. "Truly, a progressive business in a fast-growing town," concluded the Beverly News in a report on the official opening.

"The Finest Home Style Baking" was a slogan and their ads proclaimed: "Oven Fresh Bread Baked Daily. Wholesome, Nutritious, Appetizing. Stop in and get your order today, or we

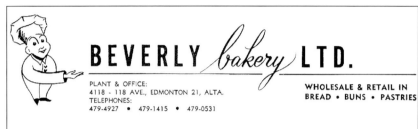

Artifact courtesy
Anton Jansen

do House-to-House Delivery." In 1972, the company introduced Quick-U-Bake products and the frozen dinner and cheese buns quickly became best sellers in Alberta retail and institutional outlets. Early in 1987 two young Italian-Canadians, Pat Rota and Santo Cardamone, bought the company and carried on the name and tradition for quality. Today, the business operates as Italian Bakery, owned by the Frattin family, and remains a Beverly landmark.

The Beverly Page

When the rumours were swirling that a chemical plant was going to built near Beverly, Germaine Dalton decided enough was enough. Determined that a vehicle was needed to keep citizens informed, the 40-year-old woman decided to canvass local businesses and measure support for a local paper. The result was the Beverly Page, which commenced publication in August 1953 as a four page publication newspaper that was distributed to 1,000 subscribers. For the first ten years, the paper was sold and distributed by carriers but, after several were beaten and robbed, the paper went to free distribution.

Germaine Dalton, Publisher of The Beverly Page

Provincial Archives of
Alberta, Edmonton Journal
Collection J4367/2

Over the next three decades, Dalton and her son Marcel built the community paper into a thriving publication with seven employees and 21,000 subscribers. "It gave us a good living," Germaine said in a 1978 interview on the occasion of the paper's 25th anniversary. "It sent my three boys through university." Since 1978, the paper has been run by son Marcel. The Beverly Page wasn't the first community paper to be published in the town; The Ladder and the Beverly Advertiser were both published in the days before the Depression.

Bay Drugs Car, May 1957

Photo courtesy Stella Baydala

Bay Drugs

3902 118 Avenue

Walter and Stella Baydala moved to Beverly in the spring of 1955 and started their Bay Drugs, a pharmacy that was to become a local landmark. The couple recalls that after considering several locations, they decided on a space at the corner of 118th Avenue and 39th Street. "I recall that we rented the space from Louis Bury and that we weren't sure that we could make ends meet, seeing as that we had no money and one small child. We opened up Bay Drug with some loans from our families and with a lot of hard work, we managed to stay afloat."

In 1960, the Baydalas sold the drug store to Ron Helland and moved to Swan Hills. Three years later, they moved back and settled again in Beverly. Their Baydala Drugs on Jasper Avenue and 103 Street became a downtown fixture for many years.

Clover Bar Saddlery, circa 1967

Photo courtesy
Roy McCoughey

Clover Bar Saddlery

4520 - 118th Avenue

This well known Beverly landmark was constructed in 1962 from a part of local Edmonton history. The rafters for the structure came from the bleachers that were put up for the 1939 Royal Visit of King George VI and Queen Elizabeth (the Queen Mother). Until the building burned down, those who looked carefully could even spot the bleacher numbers.

Beverly's First Doctor

It wasn't until 1957 that Beverly got its first resident doctor - a general practitioner named Mel Snihurowych who hung his shingle on November 1st. He rented space in the old Bay drugstore, which he recalls as a limited space with just one window. The good doctor had to put in some partitions to separate the waiting and examining areas and he remembers having to install a fan to get a breath of air. "It didn't help very much," he shakes his head. Dr. Snihurowych built his own office across the street in 1965 and remained in practice until he had a stroke in October 1993.

Other prominent 1950s businesses included The Embassy Club, Beverly Hardware, Beverly Bridge Service Station and North Star Oil Garage and the Denney Department Store (later Beverly Variety).

City of Edmonton Archives

The Beverly Crest Motor Hotel

3414 118 Avenue

The 1960 announcement of the planned construction of a new hotel between 34 and 36 Streets along the northside of 118 Avenue generated much excitement in the community. The new hotel was to supply a minimum of 20 new jobs. Owned by brothers William and Joe Lutsky and "Wolfy" Margolis, the Beverly Crest Motor Hotel was completed in 1961 and the official opening came the following spring. "It wasn't an easy time, the hours were long and the work was hard," Joe recalls. "But I guess we did alright."

Designed by the Edmonton architectural firm Hemingway and Laubental, the 42-room hotel was acclaimed for its extensive use of plate glass, which lent the lobby an "air of spaciousness," according to one newspaper account. "The hotel is designed as far as possible on one level," the article continued, "the exception being the downstairs banqueting rooms and one floor of bedrooms on the second floor reached by a wide, gently rising staircase. The design has thus eliminated the necessity of elevators, a necessary convenience in most hotels."

Travelodge Beverly Crest, May 2000

Each room featured low dressing tables crafted in walnut, a full-length wall mounted mirror and a full size double bed and a duo-bed lounge. An advertisement announcing the official opening urged readers to "see the exciting modern decor of the Firebird Room, the Crest Coffee Shop, dining room and beverage rooms. Popular country music star Gaby Haas and his group played from two until five opening afternoon and the event was broadcast live on CFRN Radio. Instead of pictures, every room boasted a wall mural. The general contractor was K. Vollan Limited, the Edmonton firm that also built many Beverly schools during the 1950s.

From the beginning, the hotel was known by locals as "The Crest." Over the years, it has been renowned for its entertainment, its smorgasbord and its friendly community atmosphere. Lorraine Trudeau started working at the hotel in 1962 and she remembers the early days with fondness. "It was such a busy time; there were just 42 rooms then and the banquet business was very good. You got to know people because they came back again and again."

Ernie Mekechuk came on the scene as manager in 1976 and he and a new group of investors launched a $3.2 million expansion the next year. The project, completed in 1978, added 50-rooms, expanded the existing amenities and upgraded and redecorated the rooms and common areas. "We brought the expansion in just at the right time because business was booming," Mekechuk recalls. "But then the Yellowhead Highway bypass was completed and business fell off in a big hurry." Now flying the Travelodge banner, he's contemplating a further enhancement of the facility to help bring back some of the weekend and holiday family travelers.

Modern Retail

In the way that the early grocers became places of gathering, so the modern supermarkets have come to be focal points in the community. Since the early 1950s, these stores have included the IGA Shop-Rite, Safeway, Co-op and IGA Garden Market. The boom years of the 1970s saw the construction of the Abbottsfield Shoppers Mall, an enclosed, climate-controlled shopping complex with a large surface parking lot. In recent years, as retail fortunes in Beverly have turned around, the shopping centre has been renovated and improved.

Abbottsfield Mall,
May 2000

133

Canada Creosoting Plant,
1935

City of Edmonton Archives
EA-160-572

Growth, Prosperity & Amalgamation

118th Avenue and 48th Street, looking west. Circa 1968

City of Edmonton Archives, EA-275-315

A dozen years after the Province of Alberta stepped in to take over administration of Beverly's affairs, the town regained control and, for the first time since 1936, a council was elected in June 1948. It was the start of the greatest turnaround the community had ever seen and the most significant growth since the days before the First World War. In 1949, a $3,400 surplus was recorded by the town while the school board was $7,000 in the black. New buildings, improved roads and new neighbours were helping to put the community back on its feet.

The opening of the Drake Hotel in May 1950 was cited by town councillors as additional proof that "the boom is on so far as the Beverly district is concerned." Secretary-Treasurer Julius Summers expressed the belief that the new development would help improve tremendously the taxation situation in Beverly. "It is probable that our town soon will be a self-supporting unit," he proclaimed.

135

Councillor Zoltan Simo
1959-61.

Councillor John Charuk
1959-61.

Mayor John Sehn
1957-59 re-elected 1961.

Councillor Elmer Hanson
1953-61.

Councillor Nestor Waluk
1957-61.

Councillor Stephen Zaychuk
1954-61.

Councillor Peter Oluk
Elected 1961.

TOWN OF BEVERLY
ALBERTA

Beverly Town Council, 1961

City of Edmonton Archives
EA-16-1

Between 1951 and 1961, Beverly's population catapulted from 2,159 to 9,041 (according to the Dominion Census). Postwar prosperity, the 1947 discovery of oil near Leduc and the completion of the Beverly Bridge in August 1953 sparked a boom like the community had never experienced. As development accelerated, records were broken in most years right through the 1950s.

While Beverly's location made it an ideal place for industrial workers to live, the tax revenue from those residents just wasn't enough to make ends meet. The influx of thousands of people and traffic forced the town to fix roads, install traffic lights and erect more street signs. Police Chief Alphonsus McIlhargey and his assistant constable couldn't handle the work load and the town soon hired three more police officers. Residents complained long and hard about the lack of services, the high cost of telephone and bad bus service. It was hard to live next to Edmonton, which could afford such improvements because of its large tax base, while such local improvements were a long time coming to Beverly.

Beverly Grows By Annexation

To balance its residentially top-heavy economy, the town moved in 1950 to annex additional industrial lands to the east and north in the County of Sturgeon. The annexation of 300-acres of urban and industrial land, effective January 1, 1951, brought into the town limits all of Canada Creosoting Company's Plant area near 127th Avenue and 41st Street - the first time an industry other than coal was part of the town's local economic base. But the Board of Public Utility refused to annex to the town a portion of the Milner-

Steer 900-acre farm immediately north of Beverly. Efforts to attract industry to the town were met with little success because the municipality just couldn't compete with the Municipal Districts of Strathcona and Sturgeon.

The Long Road to Amalgamation

Right from the beginning, Beverly seemed destined to become part of Edmonton. But it took a long time for the amalgamation to happen. In the community's earliest days, residents wanted to remain a separate entity and the City determined that it would be too costly to annex the town.

At the end of WWII, a formal request was made by town administrator Nicholas Rushton to Edmonton that the City consider a proposal to incorporate Beverly within the city limits. The decision to make application to join Edmonton was made at a March 14, 1945 meeting of Beverly ratepayers. The City responded to the request saying amalgamation could not be considered at that time, but encouraged the delegation to bring up the suggestion at a later date.

Amalgamation was always a topic that got local feelings running high. At a March 1951 meeting, the Edmonton Bulletin reported that ratepayers were at "hammer and tongs" as they discussed the pros and cons of amalgamation. The session ended with a 69 to 18 vote in favour of joining the City , but not before the original chairman Charles Floden had resigned. "Mr. Floden stepped down amidst considerable heckling and interference with speakers and the chair was taken by Robert Wright, a candidate for town council in the forthcoming election," the paper said.

A Royal Commission on Metropolitan Development recommended in 1956 that Edmonton, Beverly, Jasper Place and portions of three other municipalities amalgamate. John Sehn, who was Beverly mayor at the time, recalls that the

Beverly "Caught In Squeeze" Between City, Industry Area

The problems that develop when a quiet little town suddenly finds itself wedged between a great city on one side and a booming industrial area on the other, were outlined before a royal commission in Edmonton Thursday.

S. H. Payne, a member of the Beverly town council, told the story as he appeared before the provincial royal commission investigating possible metropolitan development of the Edmonton and Calgary areas.

Beverly was developed as a coal mining town in 1914, and practically "stood still" until 1946, when its population was 1,200. *Oct 15, 1954*

Today, its population has soared to 5,000, its main street is an arterial highway connecting the City of Edmonton with the sprawling industry of the Strathcona Municipal District, and its town fathers are wondering where they'll find the money to finance their community's growth.

While Beverly's location makes it an ideal place for industrial workers to live, according to the town council the tax revenue from residences isn't enough to make ends meet.

Beverly is well located for industrial development, Mr. Payne said, but its tax structure "frightens" industry across the North Saskatchewan River, where the Strathcona MD has lower taxes.

TAX REVENUE LOST

The residents work either in Edmonton or Strathcona. That means their employers pay taxes to Edmonton or Strathcona. The Beverly residents do their shopping in Edmonton, and the stores they patronize pay their taxes to Edmonton.

Until recently, Mr. Payne said, Beverly had no bank. It has only a small "walk-in" post office, and there is one theatre (built recently) which is never more than one-third full.

There are no major businesses, and not a department store in the town, Mr. Payne said. Until recently, there wasn't even a hardware store.

Until 1947, there was no natural gas service in Beverly, and sewer and water facilities are in the process of being installed.

STILL INDEPENDENT

The town has an agreement with the city to buy city water, at a surcharge of 35 per cent over the city rate.

While the town of Beverly believes boundaries and administration of the Edmonton area should be reorganized to bring about more equitable distribution of costs, it doesn't want to lose its independence.

"We never did favor unconditional surrender to the city of our right to look after ourselves," Mr. Payne said.

Beverly has had a history of financial problems, according to the submission of Mr. Payne. Until 1947, the residents did not even elect their own council.

For a number of years, the affairs of the town were run by a provincial government administrator, after the council had "given up" in despair. It still has no school board.

The industry which gave birth to Beverly, the coal mine, closed in 1947, leaving much of the town undermined and the land over the workings unsuitable for certain types of building.

The town feels that no matter what happens, it has nothing to lose, and is looking to Dr. G. Fred McNally's royal commission for a solution to the problem.

"The correction of this condition does not lie within the powers of the town, but must come from a more comprehensive authority," Mr. Payne said.

City of Edmonton Archives

need for amalgamation became more evident as the strain on the town's resources continued to escalate. "With no industry to offset the expenditures, the school board constantly requisitioning for more funds and ever increasing costs of infrastructure, we had no alternative."

Beverly's Oldest Mayor

When Charles E. Floden was elected Mayor of Beverly in March 1951, he was in his 72nd year. Floden was to serve three terms, retiring from office in March 1957 when he was nearly 78. It was the end of a long and fascinating life connected with Beverly - a life that began May 31st, 1879 in Sweden. His family moved to Pennsylvania when he was still a young boy and that is where he grew up.

Charles Floden

Photo courtesy
Juanita Williams

Floden and his half brother Fred came to Alberta in 1908, drawn by the offer of 160 acres of land for $10. They landed in Wetaskiwin, went to Leduc, and walked 28 miles west where they found three sections of land near Telfordville. He stayed there until 1912, when he found work in Edmonton as a steelworker on the High Level Bridge construction project. That same year, he took up residence in Beverly and later broke horses for the coal mines. He and his wife Selma had five children - four boys and one girl - and they lived in a house at 4002 112th Avenue.

His strongly developed sense of civic duty compelled him to serve as member of the School Board for three terms, as a town councillor in 1932/33 and then those three terms as Mayor between 1951 and 1957. When he retired, residents petitioned council to name a park after him and they did just that in September 1959, when Floden Park at 40th Street and 111th Avenue was dedicated. Floden passed away November 25, 1960, following a lengthy illness. He was 81.

The Beverly Bridge

August 18, 1953 was a big day in the history of Beverly - the day the Beverly Bridge was officially opened by Premier Ernest Manning. The Premier cut the red ribbon as gala ceremonies accompanied the bridge's dedication. It had been a 30-year journey that began in 1923 with a request for a vehicular and foot bridge and punctuated by recurring interest and efforts over the years - like in 1933 when council went so far as to pass a resolution urging the federal government to build it.

Official opening of the Beverly Bridge, 1953

Photo courtesy Dirk Krol

The bridge put the town on Highway 16 - central Alberta's major east-west thoroughfare - and, with oil refineries and chemical plant springing to life across the river in the County of Strathcona, traffic on 118th Avenue catapulted to new highs. New businesses sprang to life; and homes filled long vacant lots. By the time the bridge was twinned in 1972, Beverly was a thriving community.

Services Come to Beverly - At Last!

While most of the Edmonton area boasted municipal services such as power, gas and municipal water and sewer by the 1920s, it wasn't until the boom days after the Second World War that such infrastructure began to find its way into Beverly. Calgary Power began stringing power lines in 1947 and by the end of the year electricity was available to much of the town. Natural gas arrived at the same time and then, in 1953, construction began on a much talked about water and sewer system. In November 1953, Mayor Charles Floden turned the sod to mark the commencement of construction at property along 34th Street once belonging to Jacob Prins.

Crews from Dominion Construction Company worked to install the lines for the better part of the next two years, ripping up roadways and making already difficult travel even worse.

When the well at the Town Hall was demolished in May 1954, it was headline news in the local paper. The well had been a landmark for 40 years, but with the connection to the City of Edmonton municipal water system, it was no longer necessary. However, residents had to dig deep to pay for this new luxury of running water: Beverly consumers paid 35 per cent over city rates for water. Door-to-door mail delivery, another Canadian tradition that had long bypassed Beverly, finally commenced during September 1957.

Stories of the construction of the lines and the conditions encountered by the crews are legendary. Crews arrived one morning to work on the section along

Ada Boulevard to discover, much to their chagrin, that their huge backhoe had disappeared. Thinking it had been stolen, one worker ran to call the police and several minutes passed before another crew member found the backhoe - at the bottom of a quicksand pit along the bank below the boulevard.

Beverly Town Hall, circa 1968

City of Edmonton Archives, EA-20-5109

A Building Boom

In 1954, records were broken in nearly all departments. The population catapulted over 4,000 and school enrolment topped 700. A $175,000 extension to the sewer and water system was completed in 1955 and by early 1957, more than 100 new citizens were pouring in every month, placing ever more strain on the infrastructure. Beverly was called one of the fastest growing towns in Alberta. The population in 1958 topped 8,250. During 1960, Beverly completed 14.8 miles of sidewalk construction, 19.6 miles of curbs and gutters and 2.04 miles of paving on 118 Avenue, 38th and 50th Streets.

A $2.5 Million Development Program

The biggest development and construction program Beverly had seen in its history was started in 1960, with the town launching an ambitious program of street paving, curb, gutter and lighting improvements. The work included 19.6 miles of curbing and guttering, 14.8 miles of sidewalk, two miles of pavement on 118th Avenue and 38th and 50th Streets and grading and levelling of seven miles of back alleys. Under a $28,000 agreement with the city, Beverly's sewer system was cleaned, with crews discovering 80 per cent of the sewers were blocked. The blockages were attributed to "improper care."

Beverly Has Building Boom

Oct. 17, 1957

The town of Beverly is experiencing what officials believe is the biggest building boom in the town's history. Value of building permits issued to date this month total $348,600, more than four times the total of $79,350 for the corresponding period last year.

The unusual activity which includes permits for 35 homes, one store and four garages issued this month, is attributed to the $150,000,000 made available by the federal government through the Central Mortgage and Housing Corporation for construction of low-cost housing.

Construction firms were able to start work on all 35 new homes this fall.

"A good deal of money," secretary-treasurer Joseph Batty says, "was obtained for construction in Beverly through the corporation."

Mr. Batty believes the "remarkable increase" in construction this year marks "the greatest period of growth in building and population the town has ever known."

City of Edmonton Archives

To complete the roadway work on 118th Avenue, the main thoroughfare was closed for more than five weeks beginning October 1st, 1960. Business owners were not impressed. The street was barricaded from 35th Street to 50th Street and traffic detoured north along 119th Avenue as the street was leveled to engineering standards, graded, a base of concrete poured and then topped with concrete and asphalt. Edmonton Commissioner Dudley Menzies, visiting Beverly on business, was quoted in the Beverly Page as being absolutely stunned at the way all streets were barricaded, making it practically impossible for any outsider to find his way around town. After all the fuss, the street opened - smoother and drier than it had perhaps ever been. The businesspeople, that had threatened to sue, rolled up their sleeves and got back to work.

A Final Flap at Beverly Council

The province's Municipal Affairs Department completed an investigation into Beverly's administration in November 1961, but opted not to release it to the press because Beverly as an entity was about to vanish and the matter was no longer of public interest. Councillor John Charuk saw it differently and released the report to the media, saying "the residents of Beverly have a right to know the full results of the probe." The investigation was sparked by a petition demanding more open governance, organized by the Beverly Business Men's Association and signed by 589 Beverly ratepayers. The report found that while the procedures followed by Beverly town council in administered town affairs were "not always business-like they are, nevertheless, not in error so far as the Town and Village Act is concerned."

For his action, Charuk was censured in a 5-2 vote by his council colleagues. The local media came to Charuk's defence, noting in a December 21, 1961 editorial that, "It is most unfortunate that the final meeting of the council before amalgamation was marred by this totally unjustified vote of censure against a man who was doing his duty."

Mayor John Sehn,
1957-1959

City of Edmonton
Archives, EA-16-3

Amalgamation

Ending many long years of wrangle over whether to join or not to join, Beverly citizens voted 62 per cent in favour of joining Edmonton. The amalgamation approved by the Public Utilities Board and was made effective December 30, 1961. There was no fanfare like signing on the dotted lines or shaking of hands by town and city officials to "close the deal" on the effective date. Instead, an order proclaiming the merger of the two centres, signed by R.D. Henderson, chairman of the Public Utilities Board, was issued and published in the December 30, 1961 issue of the Alberta Gazette, the official publication of the provincial government. At the time of amalgamation, Beverly's population was 9,000, bringing Edmonton's population to 287,000.

Edmonton agreed to absorb the 30 permanent Beverly employees into its workforce and provide utilities at the same cost Edmonton residents were paying. The city also absorbed Beverly's debt of $4.163 million on an assessed value of $8.57 million. The Edmonton Transit System began bus service in Beverly at 7 am, News Year's Day, absorbing Beverly Bus Lines Company's seven drivers. ETS announced plans to buy the company's nine buses - five of which were more modern coaches.

At the "handing over" ceremony January 5th, 1962 at the Edmonton Petroleum Club, Mayor John Sehn presented Edmonton Mayor Elmer Roper the "key to the town," the minutes of the Village of Beverly's first meeting in 1913 and of the town council's final session in 1961. At the ceremony, Mayor Sehn talked of Beverly's economic woes, which he said had become part of the town itself. "Instead of the thriving metropolis promised by the real estate promoters, one recession after another set in," he noted.

The meal that night consisted of assorted relish, consomme vermicelli, roast prime ribs of beef, cauliflower polonaise, baked potato, tossed salad with choice of dressing and assorted French pastry. For those diners "who may prefer fish," broiled arctic char was also offered.

Beverly Town Council at Amalgamation, 1962
Charuk, John
Oluk, Peter
Waluk, Peter
Simo, Zoltan
Zaychuk, Stephen
Hanson, Elmer
Sehn, John
Batty, Joseph

City of Edmonton Archives, EA-16-2

Beverly's reputation as Edmonton's poor cousin was so entrenched that the then municipal affairs minister, A.J. Hooke, asked that the city's newest community not be referred to as the Beverly district. "Let's not look upon it as a poor cousin we had to bail out," Hooke said in a January 1962 Journal article. But as Mayor Sehn said, there was no getting around the truth. While there were some hard feelings over the move to join Edmonton, history shows that amalgamation was good and bad for Beverly. On the positive side, residential taxes decreased by about a third, property values increased, infrastructure improvements cost less and schools were usually better equipped. However business taxes increased dramatically and Beverly still didn't get the services it desired. Repeated citizen requests for a health care clinic, a library branch, recreational facilities and a social services office went unheeded.

From Dump to Park

A gully and an attempt at strip mining coal in the 1950s on the Prins Farm was the beginning of the Beverly Dump. During the 1950s, the dump was frequented by black bears, which used to rummage through the garbage and provide amusement - and a few anxious moments - for locals. The landfill site, south of 118th Avenue and east of 30th Street, was purchased by Edmonton in 1956 for $30,000, heralding the start of many years trucking the city's garbage through the heart of Beverly.

The dump started as a sore point between Beverly communities and city hall and, by the early 1970s, its continued operation had festered into a deep wound. Fallout from loaded garbage trucks traveling 118th Avenue and health concerns related to smouldering garbage overwhelmed meetings between residents and city administrators and politicians. The life of the dump in 1956 was estimated by the city at 10 to 15 years and the initial plan called for the area to be converted to parkland once the site had been filled with refuse. In 1965, the original Beverly outfall sewer, which drained into sewage lagoons created from unfenced gravel pit holes directly south of the dump, was re-

Beverly Dump, date unknown

Provincial Archives of Alberta, Edmonton Journal Collection, J672

routed to the city's North East Sewage Lagoons. The landfill was then extended southward to cover the hazardous open sewage ponds. Part of the local legend of the dump are stories of those who frequented it - and even a man and his son who lived there. "You couldn't get anywhere near the fellow; he smelled so bad," long-time resident Walter MacDonald recalls. "Every so often, somebody would drive or haul an old car into the dump and it wasn't long before somebody else was in there in fixing it up and driving it out again." Many times, fire broke out in the rubbish and crews were called to extinguish the flames - a process that sometimes lasted for many hours and even days.

In the late 1960s, the Rundle Heights subdivision developed up to the southeastern edge of the original gully used for dumping and, to minimize the nuisance to those houses, that part of the dump was contoured to specifications outlined in the city park plan. In 1972, the city completed the nine-hole Rundle Park Golf Course. The park itself, the eastern gem in the river valley necklace that became the Capital City Recreation Park, officially opened in the summer of 1978, named for Methodist Missionary Robert T. Rundle. It brought an end to a smoky, smelly chapter of the Beverly story. Now, driving the undulating road that enters the park isn't just a trip into the river valley - it's a passage over the discarded past.

Rundle Park Construction, July 14, 1971

Provincial Archives of Alberta, Edmonton Journal Collection, J648

Echoes of a Coal Mining Past

Benny Bevilacqua was standing on a cement patio block in his backyard when it opened under his feet like a trap door, causing him to fall into an old shaft. Bevilacqua grabbed the sides of the hole as he fell and was able to hoist himself out. The July 1984 incident sent shock waves through the community, but cave-ins like this one have been happening in Beverly since the earliest days of mining. Maps show that most of Beverly east of 42nd Street to the bank of the North Saskatchewan and south from 122nd Avenue to the river has been mined at one time or other.

Rundle Park, May 2000

145

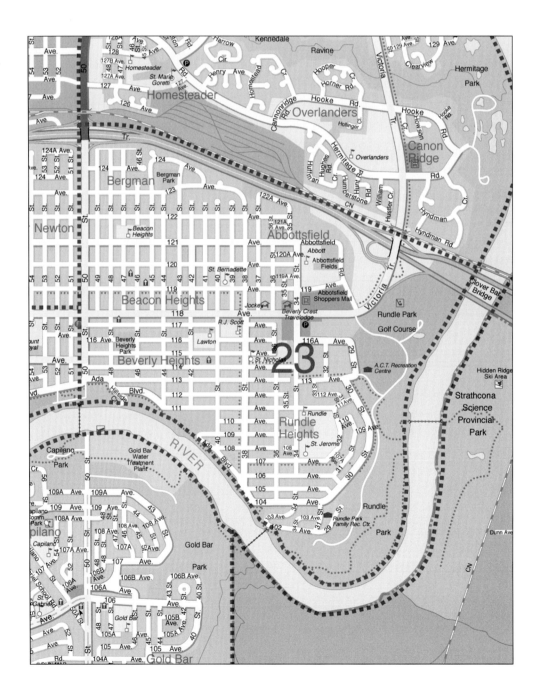

Decline & Revitalization

Section of mural by Eastglen High School Art students, completed 1998

*I*n the same way economic boom came to Beverly in the 1950s, economic bust arrived with a vengeance in the 1980s. Declining population and evolving shopping and traffic patterns devastated business and the once thriving 118th Avenue commercial district was riddled with "For Lease" signs posted in the windows of vacant storefronts.

When Beverly joined Edmonton in December 1961 its population was 9,000. Ten years later, 10,760 persons called the Beverly neighbourhoods of Beverly Heights, Beacon Heights, Rundle Heights and Bergman home. But then an exodus to the suburbs commenced and, by 1987, the population had dropped by 3,500 to 7,287. The slide continued into the 1990s.

The opening of the Yellowhead Trail in 1979 also siphoned traffic away from 118th Avenue, although city transportation statistics reveal traffic volumes were similar in to the years before and after Highway 16 was diverted from Beverly. The city approved multi-family housing projects, creating what critics called "instant slums." Built next to an established neighbourhood of single family dwellings, the projects changed the dynamic of the community and left many long time residents wondering what was happening to their little town on the edge of the big city.

To combat the decline in business and population, groups like the East Edmonton Business Association worked to launch revitalization initiatives, but met with only modest success. It wasn't until the late 1990s that Beverly began to climb back on its feet, with the opening of the Beverly Community Development Office in October 1995. When the community went before city council to solicit funding for the Abbottsfield-Rundle Heights Community Development Plan, council responded by providing $50,000 more than requested - a remarkable show of confidence. Over the next four years, the City of Edmonton contributed $65,000 a year to help fund the operation, which aimed to revitalize the community by cleaning up streets and parks, upgrading housing, increasing economic development and reducing crime.

Along with the establishment and involvement of the Beverly Business Revitalization Zone (BBRZ), the Beverly Community Development Office helped turn the tide. For Colleen Fidler and Ann Nicolai, coordinators of the Beverly Towne Community Development Office, the chance to give back something to the community was an opportunity too important to miss.

118th Avenue at 40th Street, 1998

"Beverly's always had a pride," Fidler says. "Along the way, we lost that pride and a lot of that was just propelled by sensational media reporting. But now we've got the pride back."

Now, as Nicolai notes, children of old time citizens are moving back, opting to raise their kids where they were raised. "We started to celebrate our successes and say what is good about living here. The media had been dwelling on the negative and we needed to turn that around."

The Beverly Towne Community Development Office has proven to be the catalyst for positive change and, by building partnerships with other community groups, Beverly is gradually climbing back onto its feet again. Former Edmonton Councillor Brian Mason, who represented the area for more than ten years, called it "a sort of a rebirth of a very proud community."

Beverly Farmers' Market, July 1998

Concurrent to the start of the community development project was the incorporation of the Beverly Business Revitalization Zone. After a couple of failed attempts, a dedicated group of business owners was able to convince the majority of businesses on 118th Avenue to accept an additional levy on their business taxes in support the revitalization of the avenue. A city bylaw was passed in 1995 and collection of the levy began in January of 1996. It was decided that a total of $50,000 per year would be collected from all the businesses on or adjacent to 118th Avenue, from 50th Street to Abbottsfield Road.

The Beverly Business Association, assured of an income, began work on a three year strategic plan in 1996. It soon became apparent that business owners could not volunteer all the time necessary to implement the plan and in September of 1996, an executive director was hired. Over the next few years, the business association was responsible for the implementation and completion of the first phase of the street improvements, the historic murals, improvements at the Cenotaph Park, Klondike breakfasts, a street party, a golf tournament and two area directories. They partnered with the Community Development Office and community volunteers to produce the Beverly

New 118th Avenue Street lamp, September 1998

Farmers' Market, the historic tours and local schools were involved in the Beverly Line Dance held during the Canadian Finals Rodeos. The Beverly Heights Community League sponsored the history kiosk and both community leagues, the Community Development Office and the business association formed a development committee to prevent a proliferation of undesirable businesses.

A New Life for 118th Avenue

Nowhere is the newfound pride more evident than along 118th Avenue, which was the target of a glorious $1.3 million revitalization program that began in 1997 and was completed in 1998. Four blocks between 38th and 42nd Streets were spruced up with new sidewalks and gutters, old style lamppost lights, trees with tree grates and ornamental lighting, posting kiosks and street furniture. The centrepiece of the work is a 17-metre gate bridging 118th Avenue and 40th Street, announcing "Olde Towne Beverly." Business adjacent property owners on 118th Avenue contributed about $850,000 of the bill while the city paid about more than $500,000 for roads, sidewalks and utility improvements.

"It was an enormous boost to this community because it gave people something tangible, something they could see happening and a sense of pride that, at last, something good was happening here," recalls Shirley Lowe, former executive director of the Beverly Business Association and a driving force behind the work. "These sidewalks were crumbling, and there were just seven street lights in the entire four blocks. That was fewer than any comparable commercial area in Edmonton and improvements were way overdue."

Getting people to shop along the avenue was also a key part of the revitalization strategy and, to generate some excitement, events like the Beverly Farmers' Market were launched. In the tradition of the market gardeners that called Beverly home in its formative years, the new market has found success in the parking lot of the Drake Hotel. Every Tuesday through the summer and into the fall, the market brings together vendors to sell their wares and builds stronger neighbourhood bonds. "Once you get people talking about pride of place, looking out for their neighbours, getting involved in activities, then something very positive happens," Lowe reflects. "There is a sense of community that emerges, a sense of empowerment and a satisfaction of building something good."

Just like it was for the early pioneers who founded and nourished Beverly.

The Murals

When work began on a mural on the east side of the Shoppers Drug Mart location at 118th Avenue and 38th Street in the summer of 1998, excitement rippled through the community and, just like the old days, word spread quickly. One of those who came down for a look at the work in progress was Harold Walters, who began driving truck for the Beverly Coal Company in 1938. Standing looking at the mural depicting a line of the trucks, the memories came flooding back. "We used to haul coal everywhere, because everybody needed coal to heat his or her homes," he explained.

Harold Walters in front of mural, 118th Avenue and 38th Street

The 72 foot long by ten foot high mural, the work of teacher Gene Prokop and a handful of his current and graduated art students from Eastglen Composite High School, depicts life in Beverly between 1930 and 1940. It features three families of settlers who came from different parts of the world and called Beverly their new home.

"It seems like yesterday," Steve Hnatkowski offered as he looked at the painted image of the old Beverly Central School. "I can remember one of those storm windows being carried off by the wind and right out into the schoolyard. Luckily it missed all the kids."

Mural in progress, 1998

Prokop, the son of former Mayor Marvin Prokop, grew up in Beverly and lived near 116th Avenue and 36th Street. For him the project was more than just another commission in a busy summer schedule. "We've created a mural that the community will be proud of and help people to understand more about the past." This was such a great place to grow up as a kid because it was country living at the edge of the city. We used to hunt gophers in the Prins family fields right next to our place and I have such great memories of the adventures we used to have."

Prokop wanted the mural to last and so a special wash was applied to prepare the surface and his student team used high quality acrylic paint and then sealed their creation with varnish to slow weathering and inhibit vandalism. "How can you not be energized by this kind of work," Prokop asked as his brush worked on the scene in front of the old school. "This will be here for years to come and it will touch and move people. That's a great feeling."

In the summer of 1999, the Beverly Business Association once again hired Prokop and his student art team completed to complete another mural depicting the area around the Avalon Theatre in 1950. That mural resides on the west wall of the Beacon Heights Community League, the former home of the theatre, at 4418 118th Avenue. Three more murals were in progress in the summer of 2000.

Looking to the Future

Today about 15,000 people call the Beverly neighbourhoods home. Those who live in Beverly Heights and Beacon Heights are older than the city average. Abbottsfield and Rundle Heights have significantly more teenagers than the city average, a slightly higher number of adults aged 20 to 29 and significant fewer people over 50. Bergman's age distribution is closer to the city averages but with a higher number of middle aged people.

Few buildings of its early years survive and sadly not one Beverly building is on the City of Edmonton's Register of Historic Resources. But while the face of 118th Avenue has changed in evolutionary and sometimes all too sudden fashion over its life, there are other pockets in the community that, despite the passage of years, have retained the spirit of what was long ago.

Nearly 100 years after the name "Beverly" was attached to a hopeful little settlement on the northern shoulder of the North Saskatchewan River valley, Edmonton's working class town is back on its feet again. "Everything just came together at the right time," Ann Nicolai reflects. "I feel the Community Development Office was the catalyst that got it going and helped channel the energy. But the real credit goes to the citizens who wouldn't give up and knew that if they worked hard, Beverly would one day step closer to its potential."

Mural detail, Beacon Heights Community League Hall, 1999

Appendix I

Avenue Names 104 to 118
Beverly Heights & Annex
Ada Boulevard (North)

104	Connaught
105	Franklin
106	Washington
107	Denmark
108	Buckingham
109	Windsor
110	Balmoral
111	Kensington
112	Davidson
113	Jasper
114	Knox
115	Agnes
116	Adrian
117	Normandale
118	Alberta

Avenue Names 118 to 122

118	Alberta
119	Cleave
120	Spadina
121	Westminster
122	Woodward

Street Names 34 to 50
Beacon Heights & Annex
118 Ave to 121 Ave

34	Factory
36	Henderson
37	Sharp
38	Race
39	Wilson
40	Chaplin
41	Tupper
42	Appleton
43	Mountview
44	Henry
45	Clair
46	Sage
47	McDonald
48	Brown
49	Allin
50	Hillhurst

Streets South of 118 Ave

34	Gov't Road Allowance
36	Edward
38	Beverly Boulevard
40	Caswell
42	Appleton
44	Henry
46	Sage
48	Brown
50	Hillhurst

Appendix II

At the Helm of Beverly -
Incorporation to Amalgamation

Name	Date of Birth/Death	Term of Office	Title
Robert T. Walker	Died 1936	June 1913 - December 1913	Village Chairman
Bradley E. Simpson	1870 - 1943	January 1914 - July 1914 (?)	Village Chairman
Gustave C. Bergman	1872 - 1962	August 1914 - December 1915	Town Mayor
Robert G. Hay	Died 1930?	January 1916 to 1917	Mayor
Thomas R. Dando	1867 - 1927	1918 -1919	Mayor
Frederick C. Humberstone	1857 - 1921	January 1920 - February 1921	Mayor
Robert Weir	Died 1926	February 1921 - December 1921	Mayor
Bradley E. Simpson	1870 - 1943	1922 - 1923	Mayor
Robert T. Walker	Died 1936	1924 - 1926	Mayor
Thomas E. Kinch	1875 - 1949	1927 - 1931	Mayor
Percy Benjamin Lawton	1902 - 1962	1932	Mayor
Harry Haverstock	Died 1938	1933	Mayor
Harold Gerry	1909 - 1975	1934 - 1935	Mayor
Frank Wagner	1880 -1962	January 1936 - February 1937	Mayor
Nicholas Rushton	1879 - 1952	February 1937 - June 1946	Administrator
Sidney.V. Lea	1878 - 1950	June 1946 - June 1948	Administrator
Albert Hatasine	Unknown	June 1948 - March 1951	Mayor
Charles E. Floden	1874 - 1960	March 1951 - March 1957	Mayor
John Sehn	1927 -	March 1957 - October 1959	Mayor
Marvin J. Prokop	1925 -	October 1959 - October 1961	Mayor
John Sehn	1927 -	October 1961 - December 1961	Mayor

Compiled from records of the Town of Beverly held at the City of Edmonton Archives, newspaper clippings and material provided by John Patrick Day to the Archives.

Appendix III

Beverly Population

YEAR	POPULATION	YEAR	POPULATION	YEAR	POPULATION
1910	300+	1921*	1,039	1953	2,938
1913	400+	1931*	1,111	1956*	4,602
1914	1,200	1941*	981	1958	8,200
1915	1,000	1946*	1,171	1961*	9,041
1921*	1,039	1951*	2,159		

*According to the Dominion Census

Sources

Coal mine information from "Atlas of Coal Mine Workings in Edmonton and Area," published 1971, authored by Richard Spence of Spence-Taylor. Available at the Provincial Archives of Alberta.

Geology information from "Edmonton Beneath Our Feet," a publication of the Edmonton Geological Society, 1993.

Various clippings from files and the microfilm collection at the City of Edmonton Archives.

Beverly Town Council minutes from 1913 through 1961 at the City of Edmonton Archives.

Research on Beverly railway spur lines by historian Alan Vanterpool.

The files of the Beverly United Church and church histories of other area places of worship.

The minutes of the Beverly School District, held at the Edmonton Public School Archives.

Various family and business histories, as noted in the manuscript.

Index